Natalia Whiting Bonner

Visual Guide to Creative Straight-Line Quilting

60+ Modern Designs

Professional Quality Results on Any Machine

stashBOOKS®
an imprint of C&T Publishing

PUBLISHER: Amy Marson

CREATIVE DIRECTOR: Gailen Runge

ACQUISITIONS EDITOR: Roxane Cerda

MANAGING EDITOR: Liz Aneloski

EDITOR: Karla Menaugh

TECHNICAL EDITOR: Linda Johnson

COVER/BOOK DESIGNER: April Mostek

PRODUCTION COORDINATOR: Zinnia Heinzmann

PRODUCTION EDITOR: Alice Mace Nakanishi

ILLUSTRATOR: Mary E. Flynn

PHOTO ASSISTANT: Rachel Holmes

PHOTOGRAPHY by Kelly Burgoyne, Christina Carty-Francis, and Diane Pedersen of C&T Publishing, Inc., unless otherwise noted

Published by Stash Books, an imprint of C&T Publishing, Inc., P.O. Box 1456, Lafayette, CA 94549

Library of Congress Cataloging-in-Publication Data

Names: Bonner, Natalia Whiting, 1982- author.

Title: Visual guide to creative straight-line quilting : professional-quality results on any machine--60+ modern designs / Natalia Whiting Bonner.

Description: Lafayette, CA : C&T Publishing, Inc., [2019]

Identifiers: LCCN 2018061039 | ISBN 9781617457654 (soft cover)

Subjects: LCSH: Machine quilting--Patterns. | Line (Art)

Classification: LCC TT835 .B62666 2019 | DDC 746.46--dc23

LC record available at https://lccn.loc.gov/2018061039

Printed in Malaysia

10 9 8 7 6 5

Dedication

Chesney and Brayden! I know that growing up with a mom who travels a lot for work and has to miss important events in your lives hasn't been easy. I've watched you two grow and become so brave and strong when I'm gone. You've been some of my biggest cheerleaders and so patient with me. Every time you two beg for me to buy fabric at the quilt shops or sketch out your own quilts, my little heart just wants to burst. I hope you two will always be creative and have a soft spot in your hearts for quilts.

Acknowledgments

Brad, thank you for everything you do! You are a rock-star husband who has done more than your fair share of household duties to help me live this crazy dream.

Special thanks to Kathleen Whiting for binding my quilts. You know I'd never finish anything if it weren't for your awesome binding skills.

Thank you, C&T Publishing / Stash Books. You have believed in me from the start. You have made the process great and the ride easy.

CONTENTS

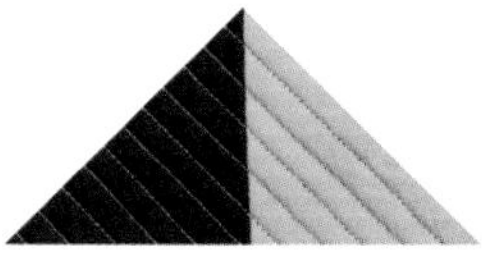

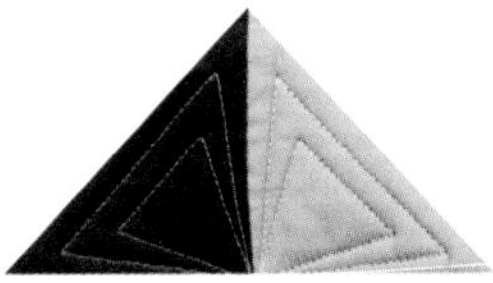

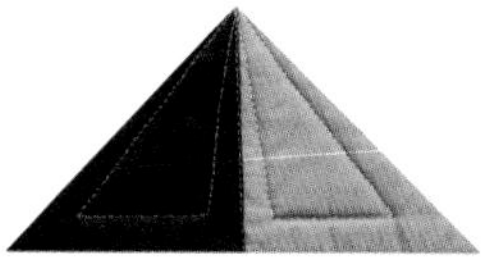

SQUARE BLOCK DESIGNS 68

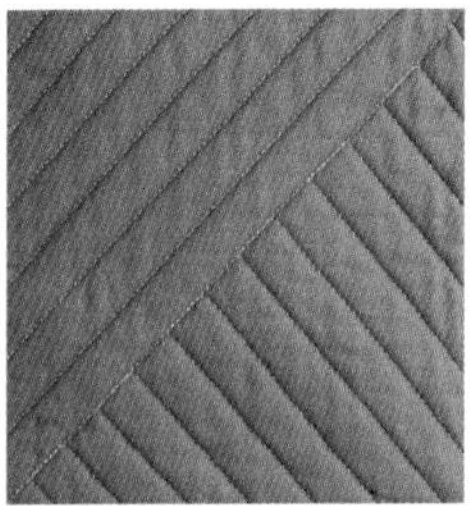

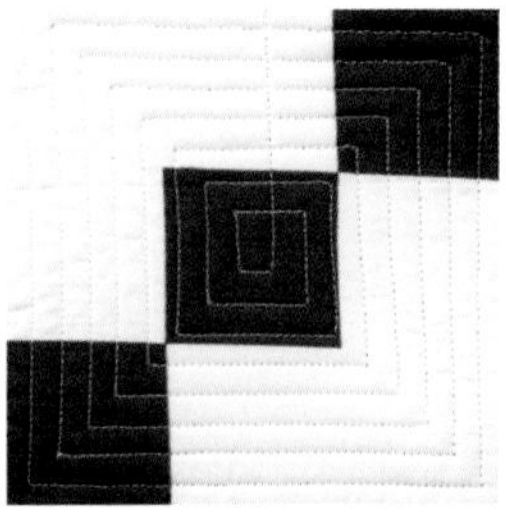

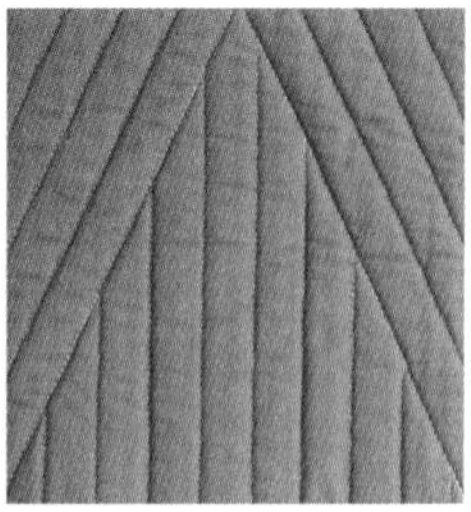

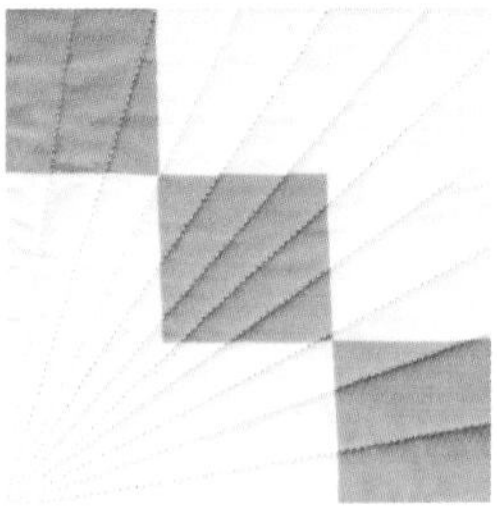

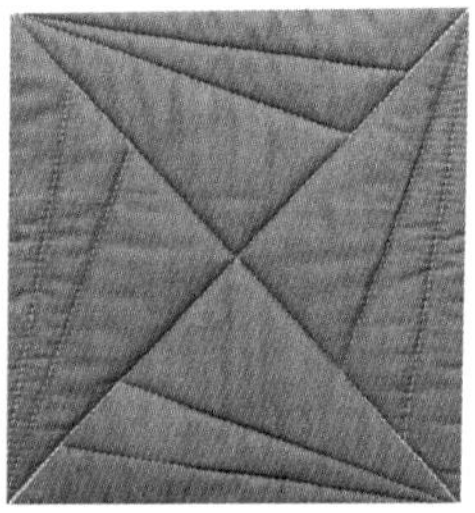

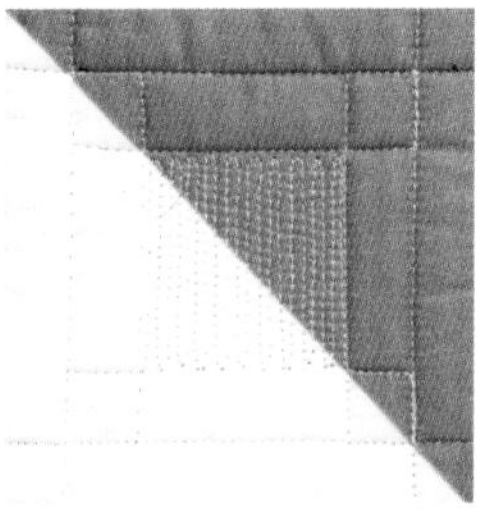

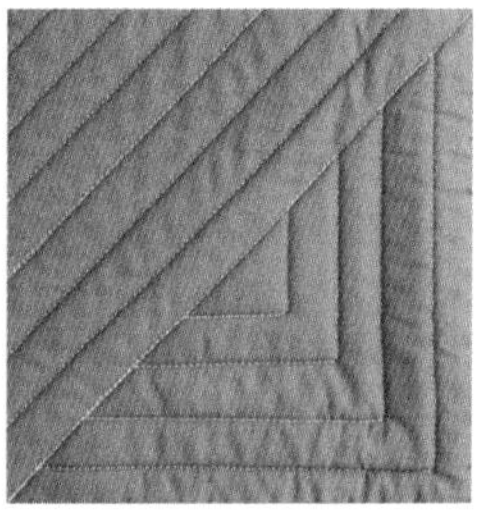

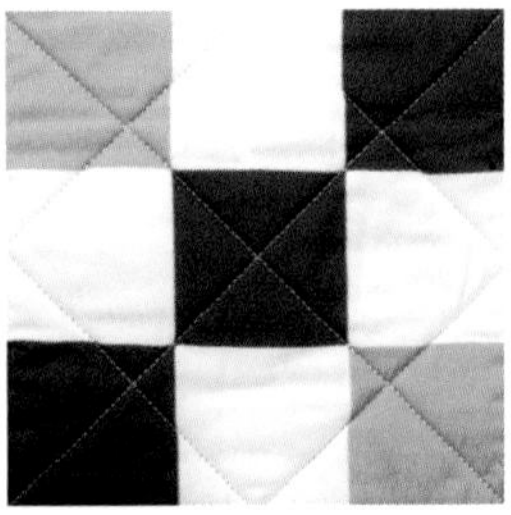

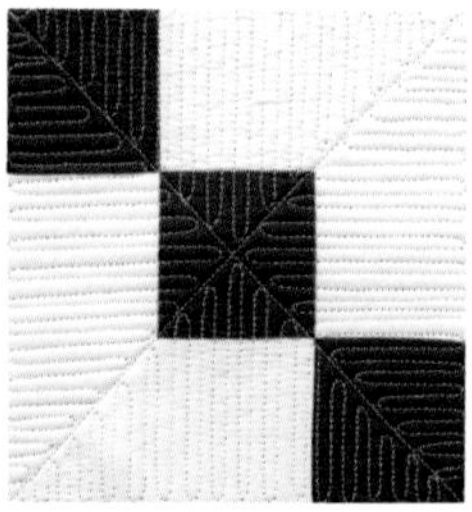

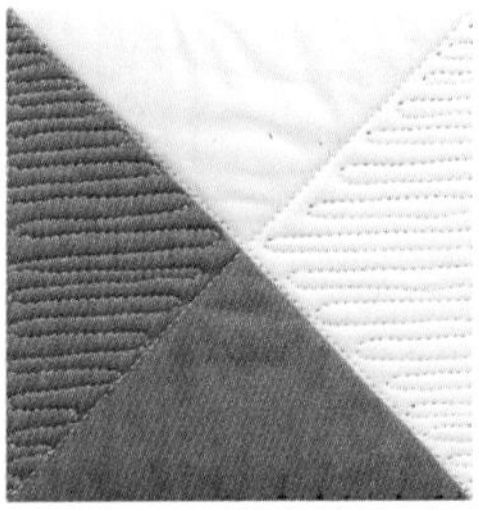

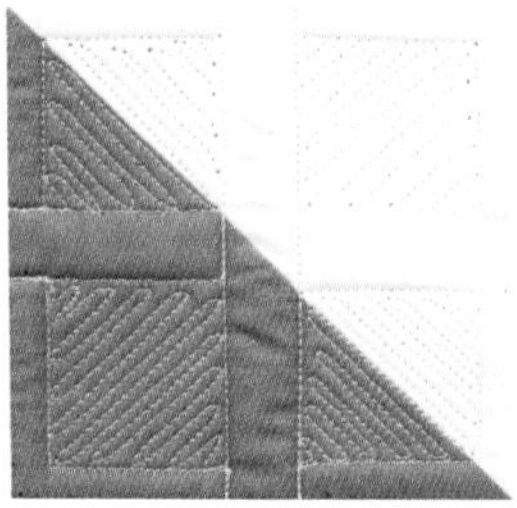

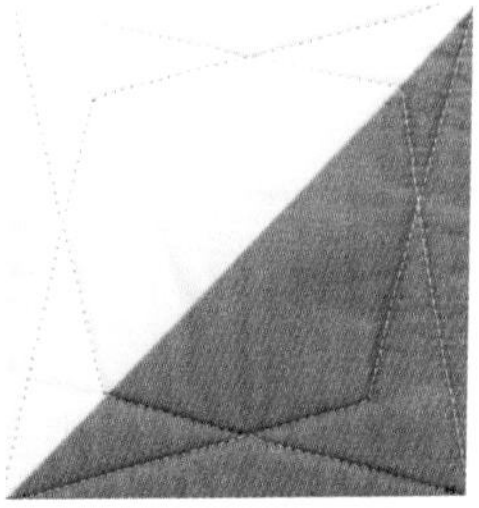

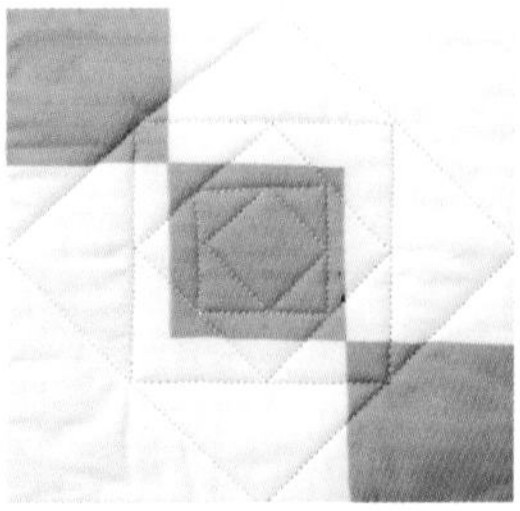

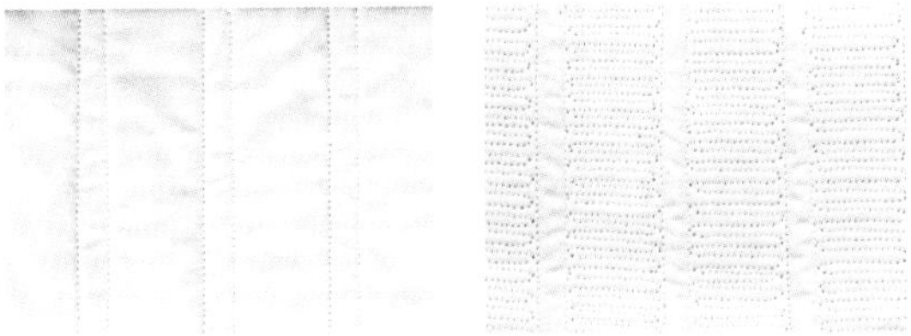

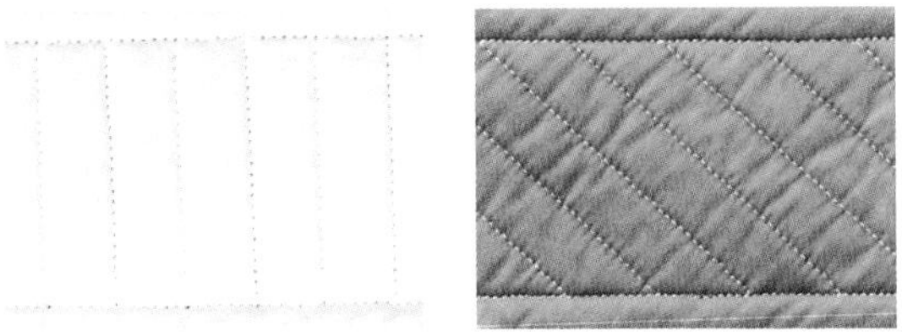

INTRODUCTION

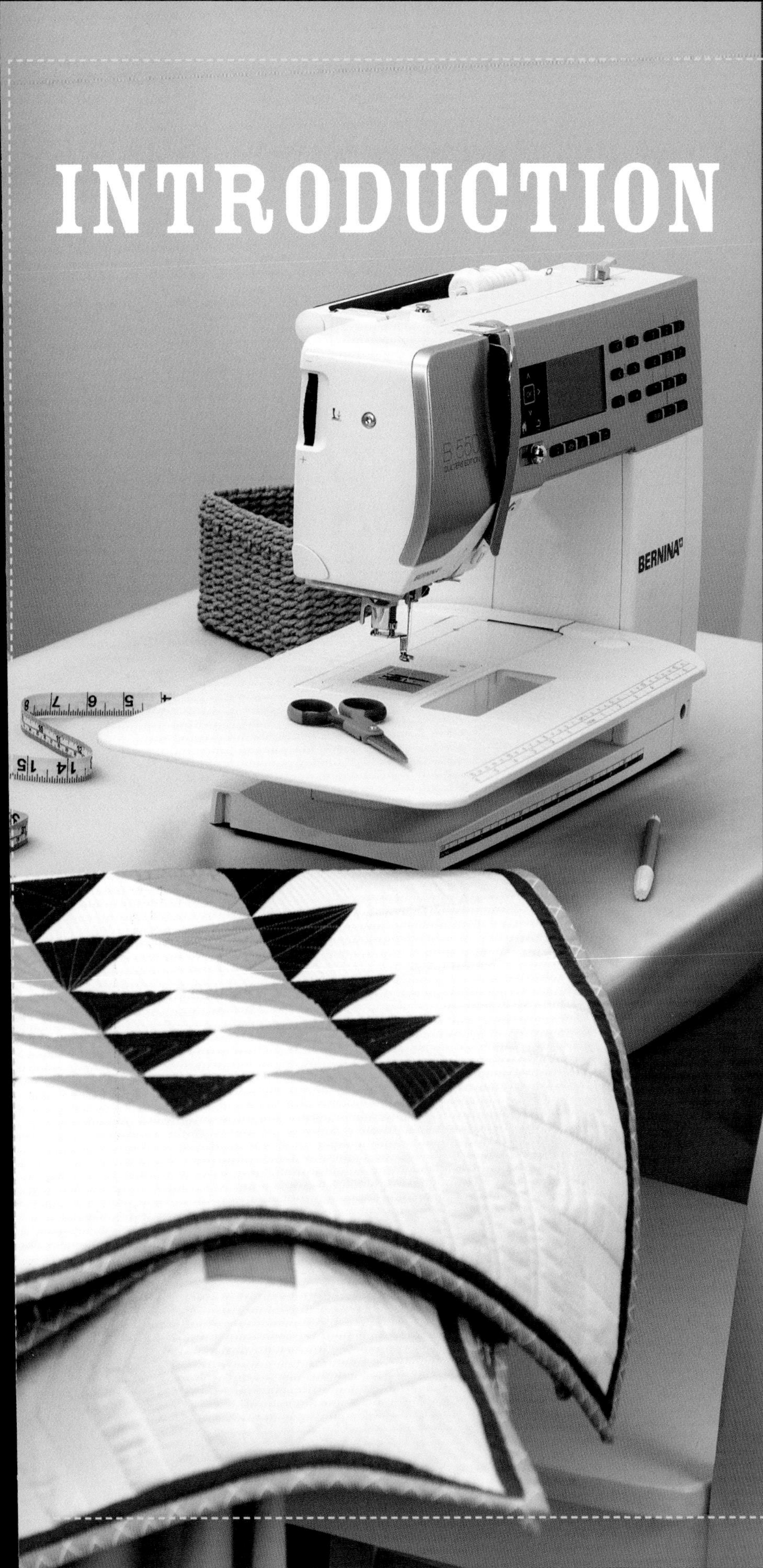

When I bought my first longarm quilting machine twelve years ago I was given a few machine quilting rulers with my purchase. Those rulers sat all nicely packaged up on the shelf for a few years. I was afraid of ruler work and honestly didn't really know what to do with those rulers.

The day finally came that I needed to use a ruler for some stitch-in-the-ditch work, and I fell in love. I realized that with rulers or a walking foot I could create really beautiful designs with just straight lines.

In this book I'll walk you, step by step, through several machine quilting designs that can be done with a walking foot on a domestic machine; with a ruler foot on a domestic machine or longarm quilting machine; and a ruler. Once you become comfortable with these designs, the sky really is the limit.

BASICS

Machine Quilting TOOLS AND TECHNIQUES

My first machine quilting book, Beginner's Guide to Free-Motion Quilting *(page 127), covered the basics in detail—threads, needles, machine feet, sewing machines, gloves, and basting. In this book, I will briefly review those tools so we can quickly move on to the exciting section, the machine quilting designs (page 28).*

FOCUS ON
QUILTING
B 550
QUILTERS EDITION
BERNINA
Free-Motion
QUILTING
Professional Quality Results on Your Home Machine
50+ Visual Tutorials
to Get You Started
BONUS
6 Modern Quilt Projects
BEGINNER'S GUIDE TO Free-Motion Quilting
SUPERIOR THREADS
SO FINE! 50
472

MACHINES

Straight-line machine quilting can be done successfully on a longarm machine or most conventional home sewing machines, as long as the machine has a free-motion foot or ruler foot and the ability to drop the feed dogs. I currently have a BERNINA Aurora 450 and a Gammill 22″ machine. It is most helpful if your machine has a large table; this accessory creates a large working area that can make it easier to maneuver the quilt under the needle and also helps to hold your ruler flat and flush against the ruler foot.

★ *Natalia's Tip*

You can buy a lot of your machine quilting supplies at my website (page 127). Look there for my 4-N-1 and Trailer machine quilting rulers, Superior Threads, needles, TOWA Bobbin Tension Gauge, and other supplies.

NEEDLES

Multiple types of needles can be used for machine quilting on a home sewing machine. The quilting needle and topstitch needle are the most popular. Each has advantages. A quilting needle has a slim, tapered point and slightly stronger shaft for stitching through fabric layers and across intersecting seams. However, most machine quilting can be done using a topstitching needle, which has an extra-sharp point and a larger groove and eye to accommodate heavier threads.

I prefer to use a titanium-coated topstitching needle. Titanium-coated needles last up to five times longer than regular needles. I prefer the needles made by Superior Threads, but you can choose from the many others that are available.

It is very important that you have the correct size of topstitching needle for your thread. I recommend three sizes for quilting: 80/12 for machine quilting with fine/lightweight thread, 90/14 for machine quilting with medium-weight thread, and 100/16 for machine quilting with heavy-weight thread.

★ *Natalia's Tip*

I always use lightweight thread with a topstitching 80/12 needle.

THREAD

Choosing the correct thread for machine quilting is very important. The most common types of thread are cotton, polyester, and polyester-wrapped cotton.

> ★ *Natalia's Tip*
>
> Never use hand-quilting thread for machine quilting. Hand-quilting thread has a waxy coating that is not compatible with sewing machines.

I always use lightweight threads, such as Superior Threads' So Fine! for the top and Bottom Line for the bobbin. But you can certainly try various threads and brands to determine what look you prefer.

When choosing thread colors, I recommend using the same color on top and bottom, especially when you are first learning to quilt. As you experiment with the correct tension for your machine, the bobbin thread could occasionally appear on the top of your quilt. If the threads are the same color, no one will notice. As you gain confidence in your machine and your quilting, you can try different threads for special effects.

THREAD TENSION

Good thread tension means that your stitching looks good on both sides of the quilt, with an equal amount of thread on the top and bottom and no loops. Loopy threads mean that the tension is too loose; puckered and pulled threads mean it is too tight.

Adjusting tension can be very tricky because you may have to adjust both the top thread and the bobbin tension. Most newer machines have a recommended tension setting for piecing but may need to be adjusted for free-motion quilting.

You can easily change the top tension by adjusting your machine's tension gauge, but it is often the bobbin tension that makes all the difference. You can adjust the tension of most bobbins by turning the screw on the bobbin case. Check your owner's manual to see how to adjust both top and bobbin tensions on our machine.

You should check the tension before you begin machine quilting and every time you fill the bobbin.

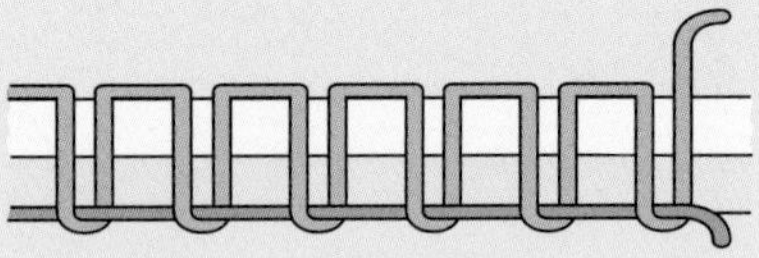

Top tension is too loose, or bobbin tension is too tight.

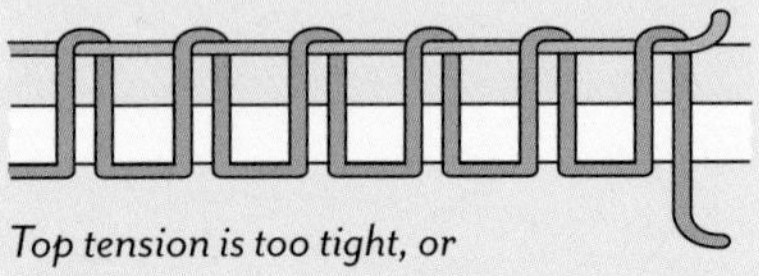

Top tension is too tight, or bobbin tension is too loose.

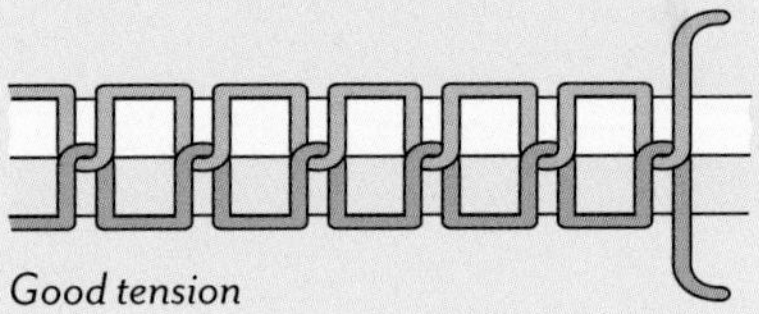

Good tension

★ *Natalia's Tip*

A TOWA Bobbin Tension Gauge is a great tool to help adjust the bobbin tension properly.

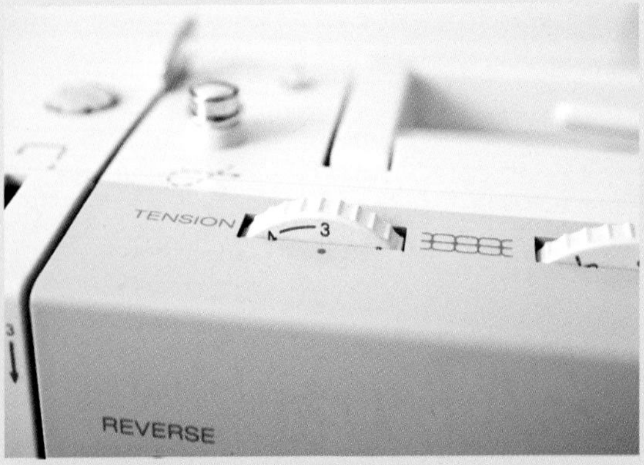

Top tension gauge

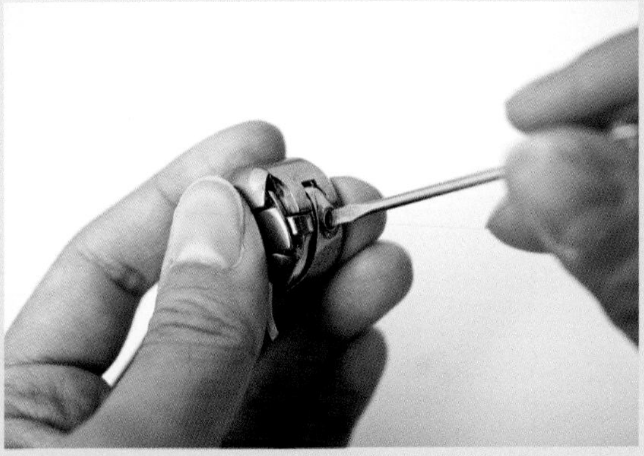

Adjusting tension screw on bobbin case

BATTING

Batting—the filling between the quilt top and backing in the quilt sandwich—affects the look and feel of the quilt, as well as the way you quilt it.

To choose a batting, you first need determine the look you want to achieve. Do you want a very flat quilt with little texture, or do you want more dramatic texture so that your machine quilting really pops? Whichever look is right for your quilt, choosing the correct batting will be a key factor in achieving the results you want.

Every batting comes with a manufacturer's recommendation for how much space you can leave between the lines of quilting (how closely it must be quilted). This can vary from 2″ to 4″ between stitching lines to up to 8″ between stitching lines. Compare the recommendation to the quilting designs you have chosen to be sure the batting will work with your design.

For machine quilting on a domestic machine, the most commonly used battings are cotton/polyester blends, which are slightly loftier than 100% cotton and a little more breathable than 100% polyester. The most common brands are Hobbs Heirloom Premium 80/20 Cotton/Poly Blend and Quilters Dream Blend 70/30. I have used and liked these, but I prefer the look and feel of the Quilters Dream Poly Deluxe or Quilters Dream Wool.

Quilters Dream Poly Deluxe, which is slightly lower-loft than most polyester battings. I love the dimension that this batting creates, and it drapes well after it is washed.

To create even more texture in your quilt, use more than one batting. When I machine quilted the samples for this book, I used two layers of batting—one layer of Quilters Dream Poly Deluxe and one layer of Quilters Dream Wool. The two battings together create a beautiful loft but are not too heavy.

★ *Natalia's Tip*

If you use two battings in the same quilt, put the denser one on the bottom and the loftiest one (usually the wool) on top. This will give the quilt more texture on the top.

MARKING YOUR QUILT

When starting out straight-line quilting, it may be helpful to mark out the design before stitching. I like to use a blue water-soluble pen, such as a Mark-B-Gone Marking Pen (by Dritz), to draw grids and guidelines.

To remove the marks, use a squirt bottle with plain water to spritz away the markings. In some cases, the marks may have moved from the quilt top into the batting fibers. In those cases, you will need to saturate the marks and blot with an absorbent paper towel or cloth. Do not leave the quilt in sunlight or near any heat source until you are sure the markings are fully removed.

LAYERING AND BASTING

Begin by layering the quilt top, batting, and backing, and then basting them together. Cut the backing and batting 4″ larger than the quilt top on all sides. Make sure that the quilt top is squared up, the top and backing are pressed, and all threads are clipped.

You will need a large, flat surface, such as a table, clean floor, or carpet. Lay out the quilt backing wrong side up. Tape it down with masking tape. On a table, you can use clamps to hold it flat. If you are working on carpet, use T-pins to pin it flat.

Center and lay the batting flat on the backing; then center the quilt top right side up on the top of the batting. Now you can begin to baste.

There are four basic ways of basting, each with its pros and cons. No matter which method you choose, it is very important that the quilt layers lie flat and are positioned correctly. It's important to take the time to baste properly, as this will help ensure better results when machine quilting.

Spray basting You will appreciate spray basting while stitching, because you won't need to stop and take out pins or worry about thread getting caught in your machine foot. However, the spray is messy, and you need to apply it in an area with a lot of fresh air. Follow the instructions on the spray can to baste between each layer.

Thread basting The downside of thread basting is that the thread occasionally will catch in your hopping foot and interrupt your flow of quilting. The upside is that thread basting is very easy to remove and is not messy like spray.

When thread-basting by hand or machine, stitch a row horizontally, then vertically, and then diagonally across the quilt—using much longer than normal stitches—to create a single row each way. Then begin to fill in, making a grid across the quilt with stitched rows about 6″ apart to evenly secure the quilt layers. If you are basting by hand, use long strands of light-colored thread and take very generous stitches so they can be removed easily when you're finished quilting. If basting by machine, use a walking foot and work from the center out in sections to create a grid.

Pin basting The pins are reusable, which is nice. But if you're in your groove while stitching, it's annoying to have to stop and remove a pin.

For pin basting, use size #1 or #2 safety pins. Curved quilting pins work especially well. I recommend using 75 pins for a crib-size quilt and up to 350 pins for a queen-size quilt. Start pinning at the center of the quilt, making sure to pin all three layers together and spacing the pins about a palm's width apart. Pin outward horizontally and vertically, creating a gridlike pattern.

Fusible batting Fusible batting is another option when it comes to basting quilts. Quilters Dream, Hobbs, and Warm & Natural all offer a fusible batting, basted to your quilt top with a warm iron. Follow the instructions that are on the batting package. The fusible battings generally wash and wear like a regular polyester/cotton-blend batting.

Learning STRAIGHT-LINE QUILTING

All the designs in this book can be used for a domestic or a longarm machine. There are two basic ways to quilt straight lines. On a longarm machine, you'll need to use a ruler foot and a machine quilting ruler. You can use a ruler foot and machine quilting ruler on a domestic machine also, or you can choose to use a walking foot and premark some of your lines.

RULERS OR WALKING FOOT?

If you are working on a domestic machine, I recommend trying out both techniques to decide which you like more.

To use a walking foot, you can use the edge of the foot as a guide some of the time. Many walking feet come with adjustable guides to help you stitch parallel lines at various widths. Or you can premark some of your straight lines and follow the marks as you quilt. The advantage is you can use the walking foot instead of learning how to free-motion quilt. The disadvantages are that you will have to mark more lines on your quilt, and—the big disadvantage—that you will have to rotate the quilt every time you want to stitch in a different direction.

To use machine quilting rulers and a ruler foot, you will need to drop the feed dogs on your machine—so, you will be stitching free-motion, but with a ruler to guide you. This is a great way to practice your free-motion skills! And because you are stitching free-motion, you can change directions without turning the quilt. Just change the position of the ruler to guide you as you stitch in a new direction.

★ *Natalia's Tip*

You can buy a lot of your machine quilting supplies at my website (page 127). Look there for my 4-N-1 and Trailer machine quilting rulers, Superior Threads, needles, TOWA Bobbin Tension Gauge, and other supplies.

MACHINE QUILTING RULERS

Machine quilting rulers are different from rotary rulers. Machine quilting rulers are about twice as thick as rotary rulers—¼˝ thick—and the markings generally start at ½˝. The markings on the machine quilting rulers are measured from the needle, so you can measure distances between stitching lines with the ruler instead of having to mark out every single line.

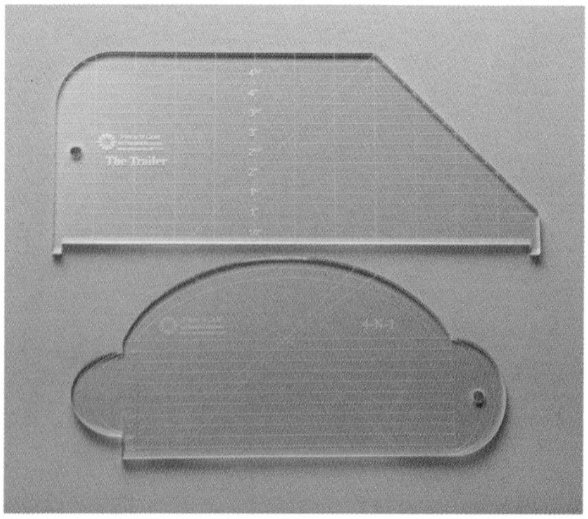

Machine quilting rulers can be used on longarm machines as well as domestic machines. If you're using the machine quilting rulers on a longarm machine, I highly recommend using an extended base plate around the base of your machine. This will create a larger working space and enable you to hold the ruler flat and flush up against the ruler foot.

When using the machine quilting rulers on a domestic machine, you will need to make sure you have a ruler foot. A ruler foot is available from your machine dealer and after-market ruler feet also are available.

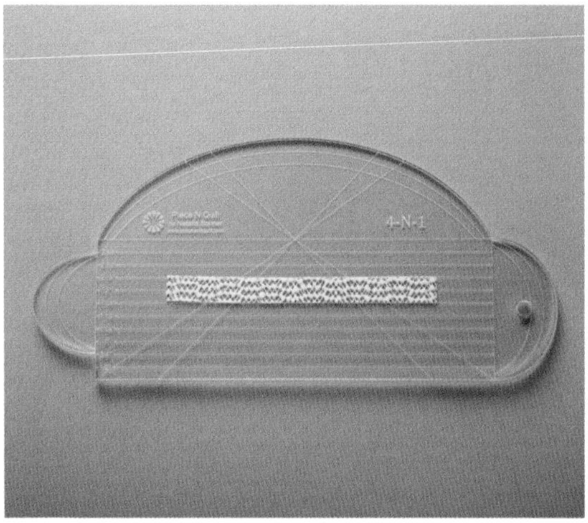

You'll also need to make sure that you're working on a machine that has the ability to drop the feed dogs and that there's ¼˝ clearance all the way around the foot.

Additionally, when working with rulers on your domestic machine, I highly recommend a grip material on the back of the ruler. This can also be used when working on a longarm machine. The grip material on the back of the ruler helps the ruler grip to the fabric and stay a little bit sturdier.

MACHINE QUILTING FEET

Ruler Foot

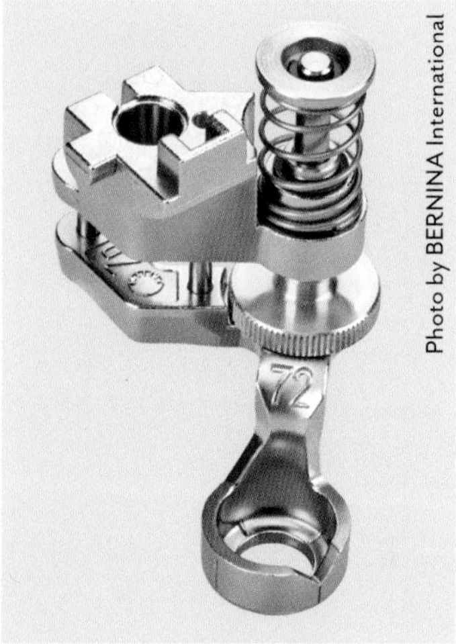

When working with rulers you'll need a ruler foot. A ruler foot is like a hopping foot, but much thicker, close to ¼˝ thick. The thick sides of the foot are made to glide nicely along the side of a ruler and help prevent the ruler from popping up on top of the foot.

The advantage of using the ruler foot is that you can change stitching directions without rotating the quilt. So, when you see the quilt design instructions say, "turn and stitch," you don't actually turn the quilt, just turn the ruler in a different direction and stitch alongside it.

Walking Foot

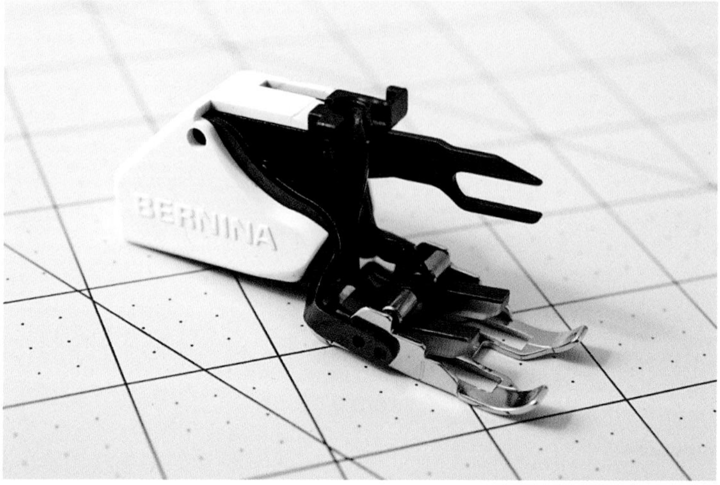

A walking foot can be used on a domestic machine to help quilt straight lines. A walking foot can be advantageous because you do not have to try and hold onto a ruler while also holding onto the quilt top. The disadvantage of using a walking foot is that you have to rotate the quilt every time you want to change directions with your quilting.

When machine quilting with a walking foot, I do not recommend using a ruler up against the side of the foot. Instead, use a rotary ruler to mark the design on the quilt before the quilting. By doing this, the design will be completely marked out and you will follow the lines that you've marked for your quilting. Follow the pattern design directions for the desired design and draw the design on the quilt.

For marking designs, I recommend using a water-soluble marker, such as a Mark-B-Gone Marking Pen, or chalk.

HOW TO USE MACHINE QUILTING RULERS

The rulers shown in this book are machine quilting rulers that I designed—the Trailer and 4-N-1 machine quilting rulers. Since these are my favorite rulers, they are what I recommend. However, most machine quilting rulers can be used in the same way.

Point-to-Point Straight-Line Quilting

Stitching a point-to-point straight line for the first time can be a little bit daunting, even with the assistance of a machine quilting ruler.

★ *Natalia's Tip*

Not all machine quilting rulers are created equal. Before you begin any machine quilting with a machine quilting ruler, make sure that you understand the markings on the rulers. The markings on 4-N-1 and Trailer machine quilting rulers are measured from the needle on your machine. Most ruler feet are circular and are created so the outside of the foot is ¼˝ from the needle. You can hold the ruler next to the ruler foot and your stitching will then be ¼˝ from the side of the ruler.

THE TRAILER RULER

The Trailer Machine Quilting Ruler is designed with little notches at the ends of the straight side of the ruler. These little notches help you see where your stitching line will end. For example, in the top right image, I want to stitch a straight diagonal line from the bottom right corner to the upper left corner. I will begin with my needle position in the bottom right corner. From there I will line the Trailer ruler notch up with the opposite corner. Now I can see that my stitching will intersect that opposite corner perfectly.

From there I will stitch, slowly, while holding gentle pressure against the side of the foot to the opposite corner. When I reach that notch, I will stop stitching with the needle in the down position, then adjust the ruler slightly so that I can stitch the rest of the way to the corner.

This ruler is also great for stitch-in-the-ditch. When stitching-in-the-ditch, you can line that notch up with the ditch and then stitch along the side of the ruler, stopping to adjust as necessary. A warning though—for this to be effective the piecing needs to be very precise.

THE 4-N-1 RULER

The 4-N-1 Machine Quilting Ruler and many other straight rulers out there do not have those little notches on the ends that help you line up your stitching lines. If you're using a ruler like this, you'll need to eyeball the ¼˝ position to ensure that your straight line will intersect the corner perfectly.

For example, in the image below, I want to stitch a straight diagonal line from the top left corner to the bottom right corner. I will begin with my needle position in the top left corner. From there I will line the 4-N-1 ruler up with the side of the ruler foot.

From there I will eyeball the ¼˝ mark and hold the ruler ¼˝ from that corner point. You may want to use your water-soluble marking pen to mark a ¼˝ increment the first few times, until you feel comfortable eyeballing the spacing.

From there I will stitch, slowly, while holding gentle pressure against the side of the foot to the opposite corner.

★ *Natalia's Tip*

I prefer to hold my ruler on the left side of the needle, because I'm right handed. I'm controlling my quilting machine with my right hand. But for best results, you'll want to learn to hold the ruler on all sides of the foot.

Measuring Spacing

You can use the markings on the machine quilting rulers instead of marking out every single point or line. To stitch out a design like the Plaid Square (page 80) or Piano Keys (page 95), begin by stitching out the first straight line. Move the ruler on top of the stitched line. If you'd like your spacing to be 1˝ apart, place the 1˝ marking on the ruler on top of the first stitched line. Hold the ruler securely on top of that line while you stitch the second line.

When using the ruler for measurements, make sure that your ruler measurements are based on your needle position. If they are not, you may want to put a piece of washi tape on the ruler to help indicate where you'd like your spacing to be.

STRAIGHT-LINE QUILTING DESIGNS

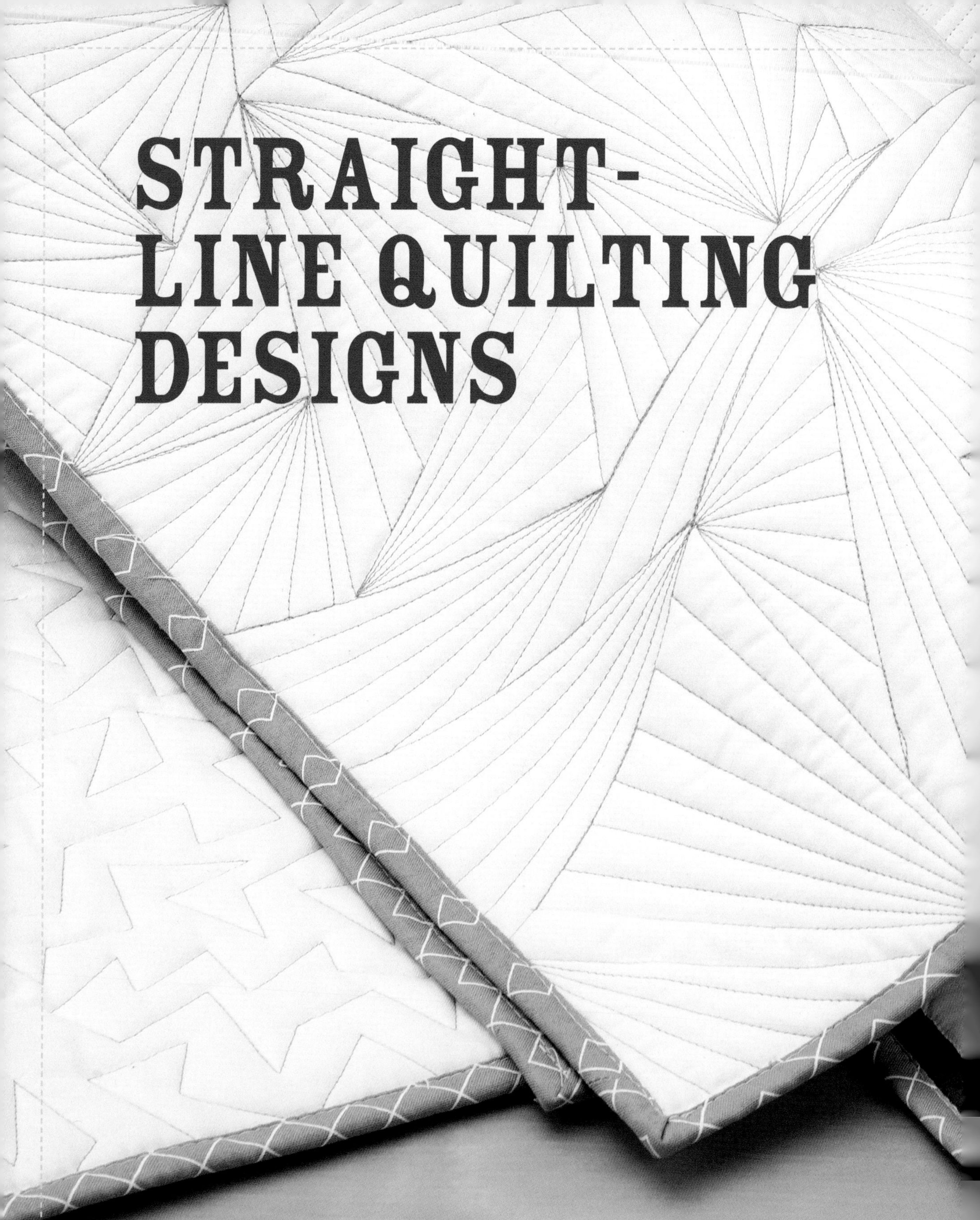

Triangle BLOCK DESIGNS

When I look at a quilt and start to decide what I'm going to quilt, I always try to look at shapes. For example, when I look at a square, I might try to break it down into two triangles or even four triangles. When I see a quilt block that is four triangles pieced together to create a square, I could treat my machine quilting like it's four triangles or as a large square.

RAYS

Rays are a great way to add detail to a triangle quilt block. This design could be dressed up if you added heavy fillers to every other open space.

STEP 1 • *Use a blue water-soluble pen to mark dots every ½˝ along the bottom side of the block.*

STEP 2 • *Beginning at the first marked dot in the lower left corner, stitch a straight line to the top point of the triangle.*

STEP 3 • *From the top point, stitch a straight line to the second marked point at the bottom left. Travel across the bottom of the block to the third marked dot.*

STEP 4 • *From the third marked point, stitch to the top of the block and then down to the fourth marked point. Repeat previous steps, stitching along the bottom edge of the triangle and back to the top point until you have filled in the block completely.*

Once you've stitched all the straight lines, stitch-in-the-ditch all the way around the triangle.

1

2

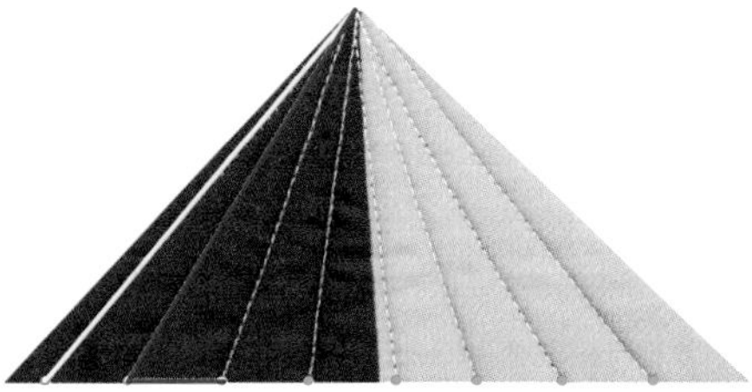

3

4

BOOMERANG

The Boomerang is a fun design for any triangle quilt block. This design is simple but can be dressed up to really create a beautiful block. The sample block is about 3˝ tall. If you're quilting this design in a larger or smaller block, you may want to add more or fewer boomerang lines.

STEP 1 • *Mark a straight line through the center of the block using a blue water-soluble pen.*

STEP 2 • *Measure through the center of the block, along the straight marked line and mark two intersection points. Based on the size of my block, the bottom marking will be about 1˝ from the bottom of the block and the top marking will be about 1˝ above that.*

1

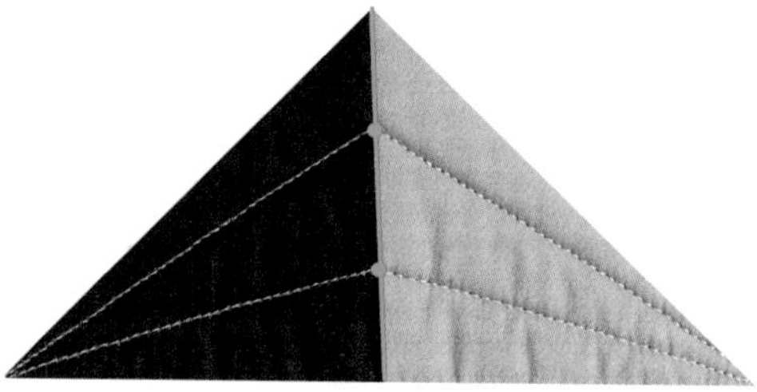

2

★ *Natalia's Tip*

At this point you could mark the boomerang lines, to show exactly where your machine quilting will go. I like point-to-point type quilting, so I'll often mark only the points in Steps 1 and 2.

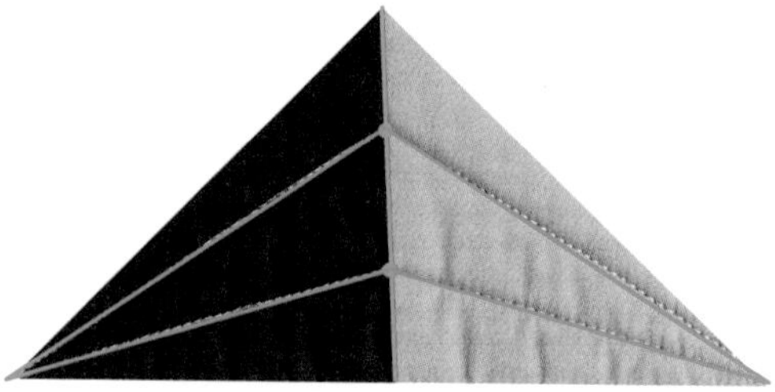

STEP 3 • *Beginning in the lower left corner, stitch a straight line to the bottom marked point then to the bottom right corner.*

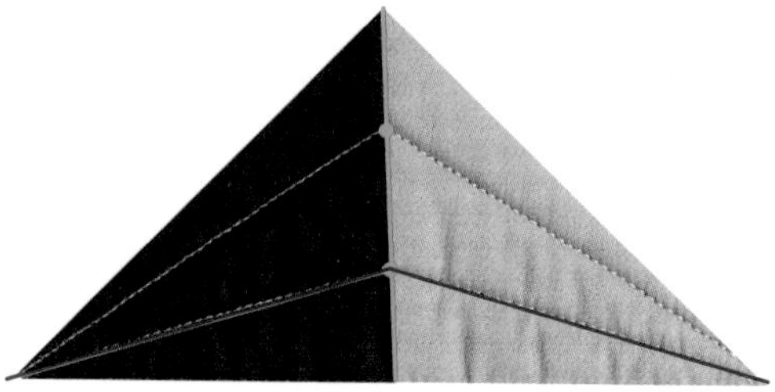

3

STEP 4 • *From the bottom right corner, stitch a straight line to the center top marked point and then to the bottom left corner.*

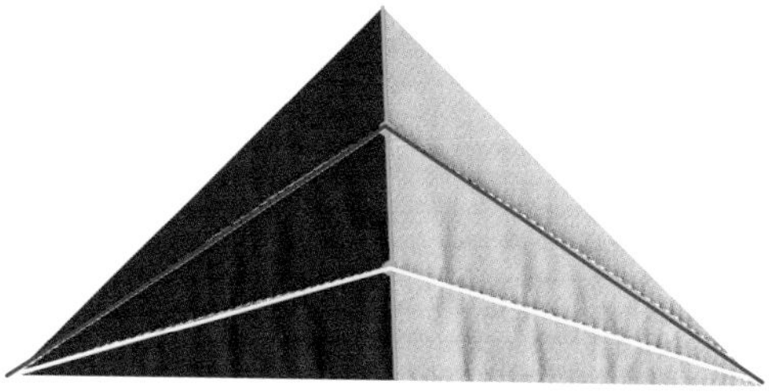

4

★ *Natalia's Tip*

I like the look of stitch-in-the-ditch, so after I've stitched out my design I'll stitch-in-the-ditch all the way around the triangle to finish off the block nicely.

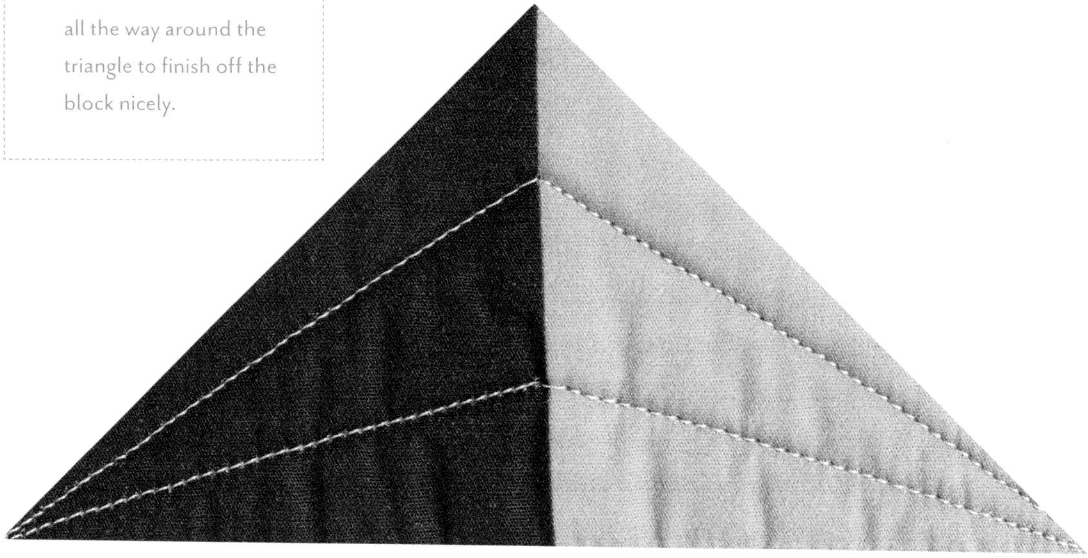

Boomerang Variation

Add back-and-forth straight lines to create more texture within the design.

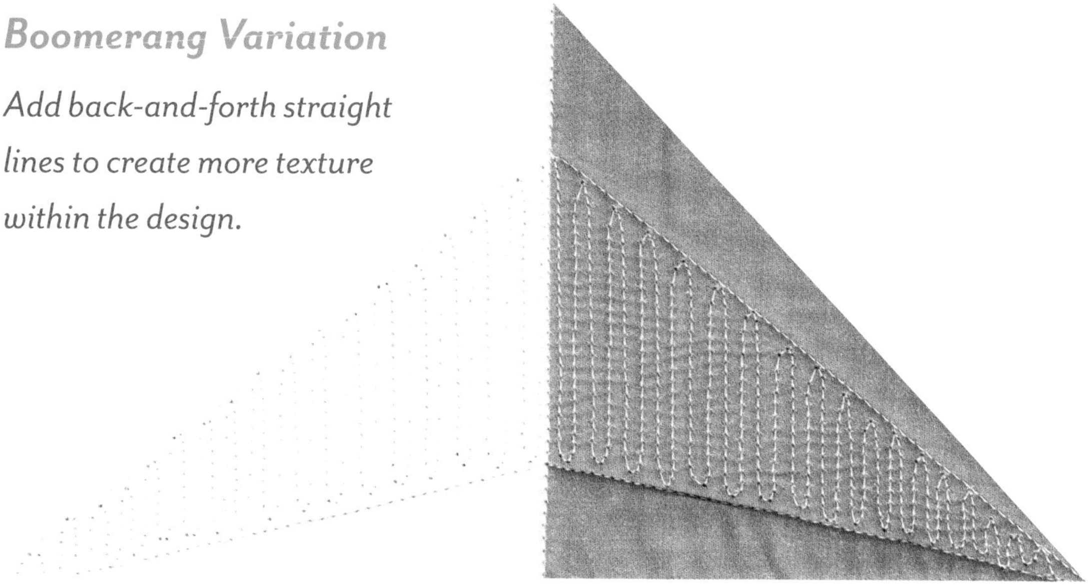

INSIDE ECHO

The Inside Echo is a simple design that plays off the straight lines of the piecing. The secondary designs that come to life with the machine quilting really create so much interest. To add even more interest to this design, fill in the open center with a fun filler like swirls, pebbles, or even matchstick quilting.

STEP 1 • *Start at the lower left corner, use the side of the machine quilting ruler to stitch a straight line to the top right side of the block. On a small block, these lines will be about ¼˝ from the side of the block. If your block is larger, keep those lines about ½˝ from the side of the block.*

STEP 2 • *From the upper right point, stitch along the ditch to the top of the triangle. Turn and stitch down the left side of the triangle about ¼˝. From that point, use the side of the machine quilting ruler to stitch a line to the bottom side of the block.*

STEP 3 • *From the lower right point, stitch along the ditch to the bottom right corner of the triangle. Turn and stitch up the right side of the triangle about ¼˝. Use the side of the machine quilting ruler to stitch a line to the left side of the block. Stitch-in-the-ditch to complete the design.*

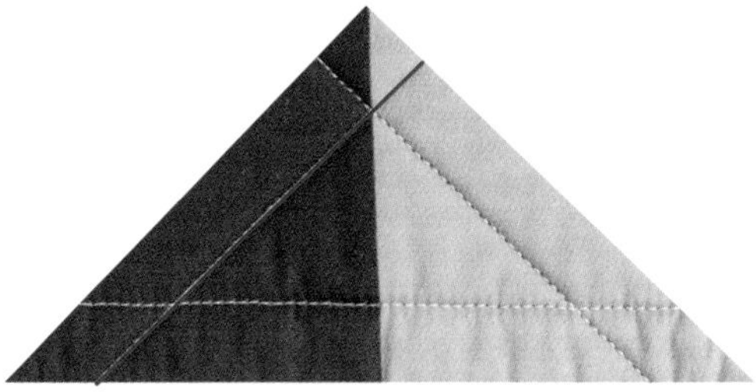

1

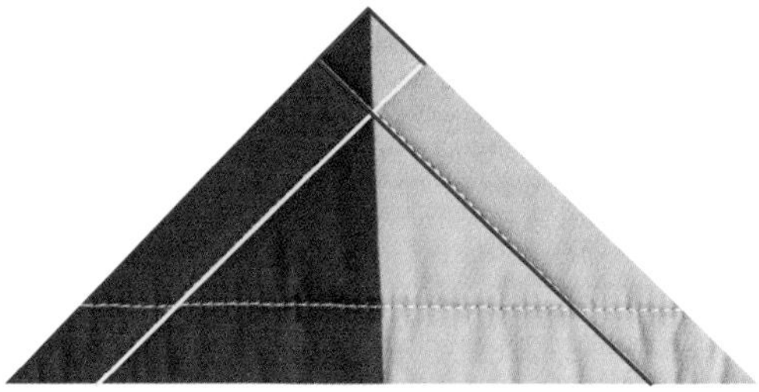

2

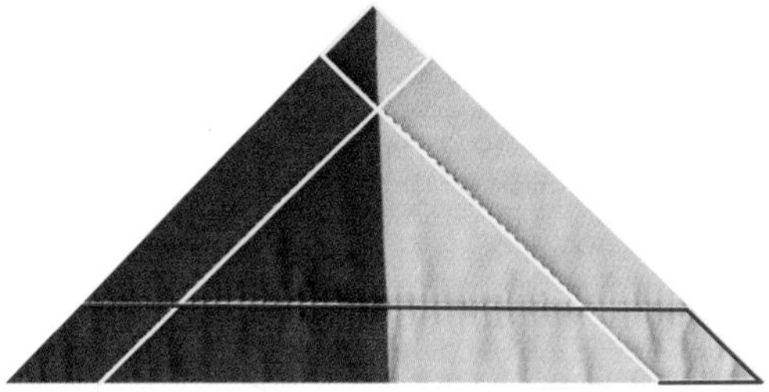

3

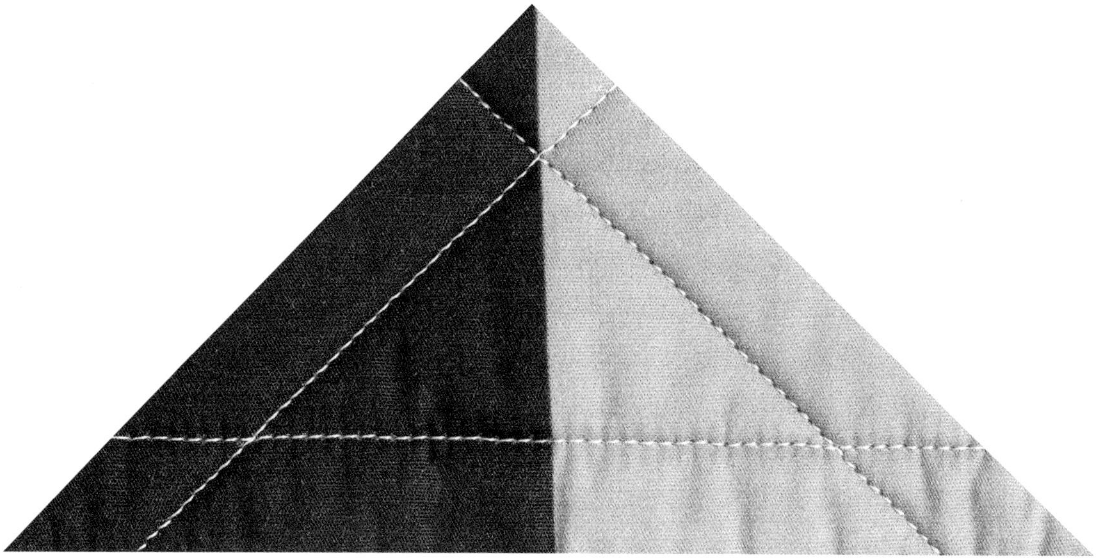

Inside Echo Variation

This variation is quilted in exactly the same way as the Inside Echo design, it's just worked inside a smaller triangle this time.

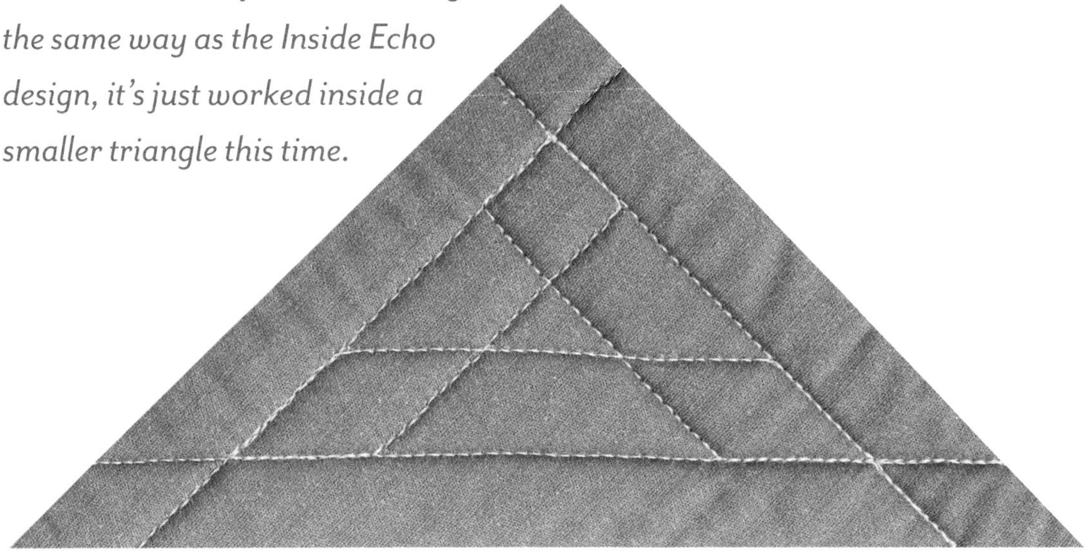

ANGULAR CROSSHATCH

I love the mix of modern and traditional in this design. When stitching out this design, you can mark out all the points, or you can use the markings on your machine quilting ruler to quilt the design with no markings at all. This design is stitched out on a 3˝ triangle, so the spacing is smaller. If you are stitching this out on a larger triangle, you'll want to adjust your spacing or add in more crosshatching lines accordingly.

STEP 1 • *Measure along the right and left sides of the block. Use the blue water-soluble pen to make 3 marks—1 in the center, then another between the center and each of the triangle points.*

STEP 2 • *Beginning in the lower left corner, stitch a diagonal line to the bottom right marked point.*

STEP 3 • *From there, stitch up the ditch to the second marked point. Turn and stitch to the lower left corner.*

STEP 4 • *From the lower left corner, stitch a straight line to the top right marked line.*

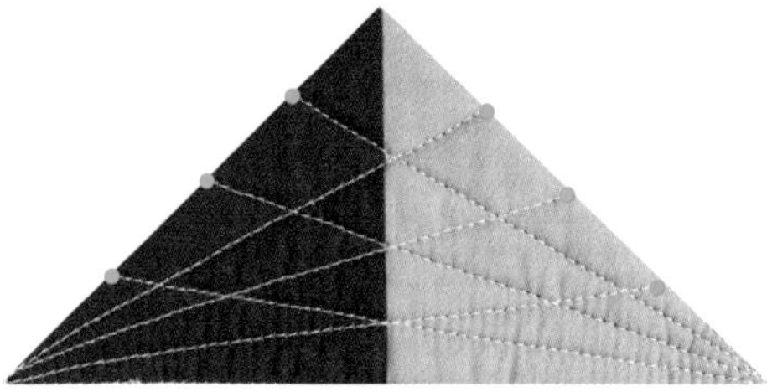

1

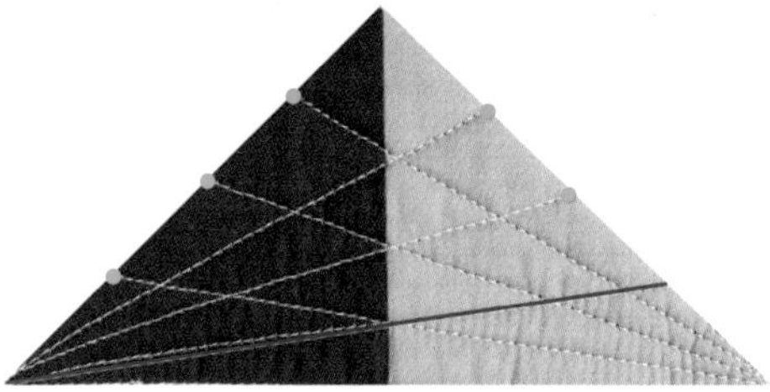

2

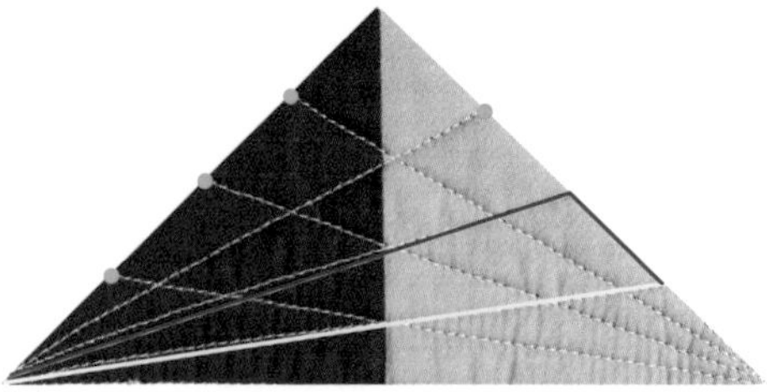

3

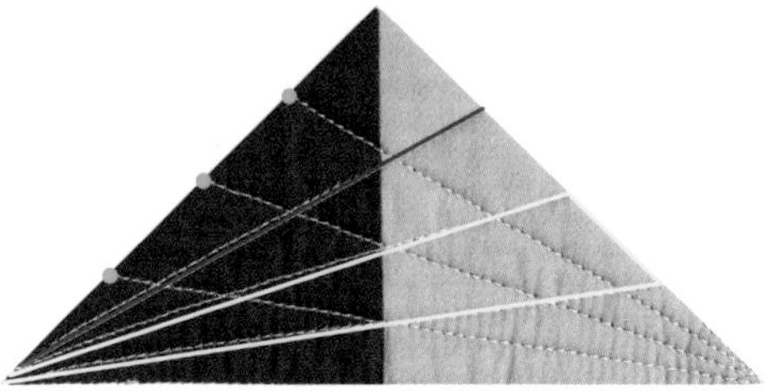

4

STEP 5 • *From the upper right point, stitch-in-the-ditch to the bottom right corner. Then from the bottom right corner begin repeating the same process stitching to the bottom left marked point and working your way, point-to-point through the block design.*

STEP 6 • *After you reach the marked point on the upper left, stitch-in-the-ditch around the triangle quilt block.*

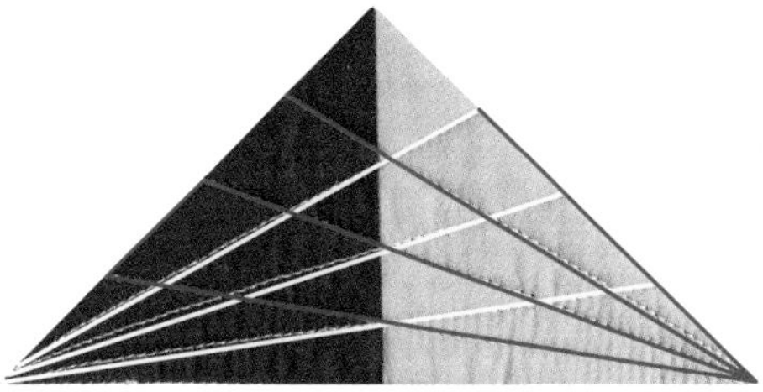

5

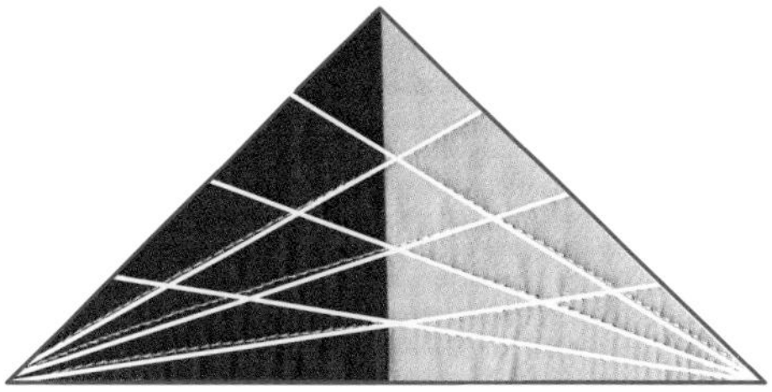

6

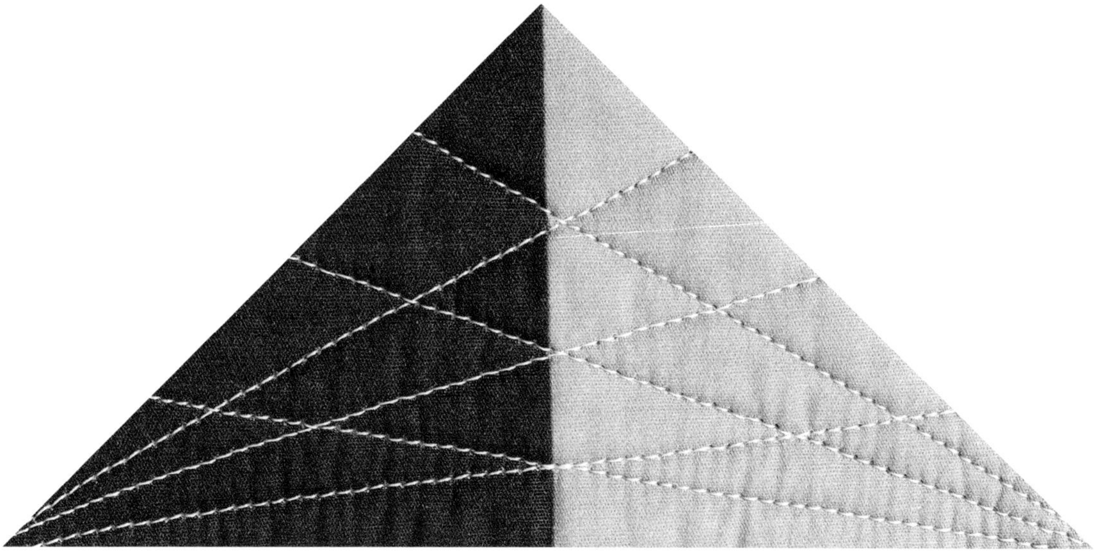

THREE-POINTED STAR

This design is beautiful stitched as a straight-line design, but it also could be interesting with a heavy filler quilted in the inside or outside shapes.

STEP 1 • *Use the blue water-soluble pen and a ruler to draw 3 straight lines connecting the center of each short side and the center of the top point to the center of the long bottom edge. Then mark a dot ½″ from the edge of the block on all 3 straight lines.*

STEP 2 • *Beginning in the lower left corner, stitch to the bottom center point, then to the lower right corner.*

STEP 3 • *From the lower right corner, stitch a straight line to the marked point on the right side and then to the top point.*

STEP 4 • *From the top point, stitch a straight line to the marked point on the left side and then to the bottom left corner.*

After you reach the lower left corner, stitch-in-the-ditch all the way around the block.

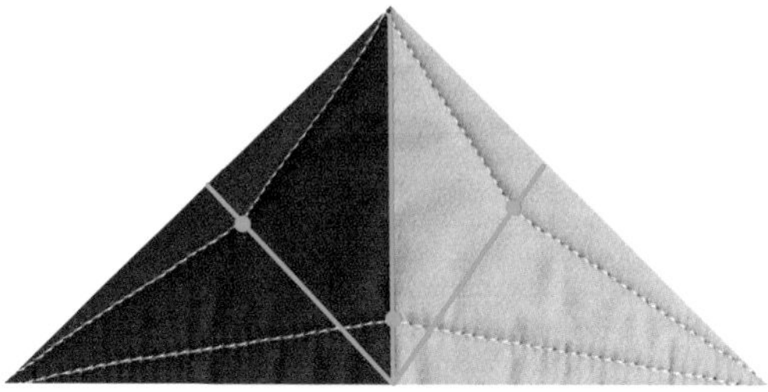

1

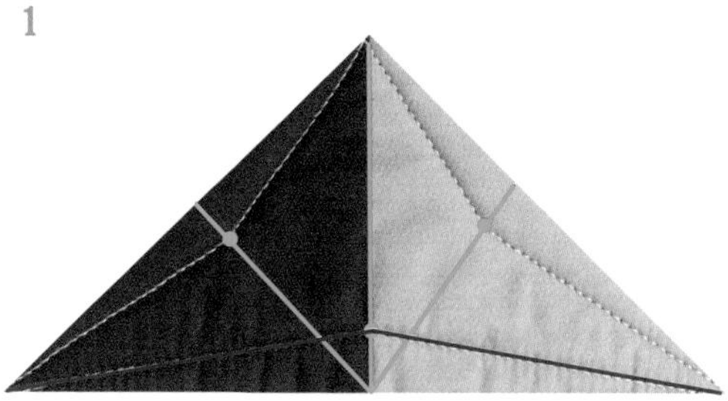

2

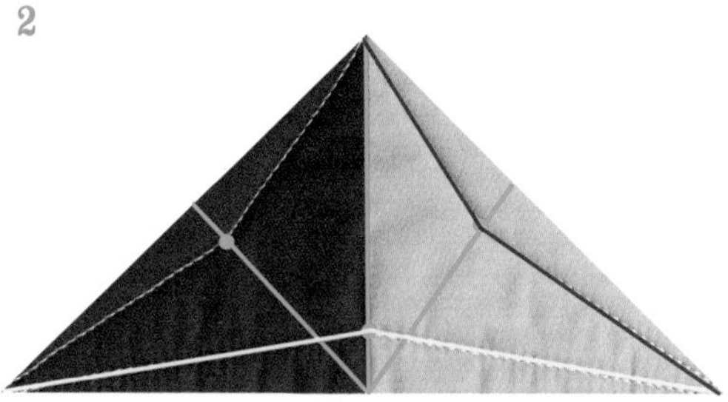

3

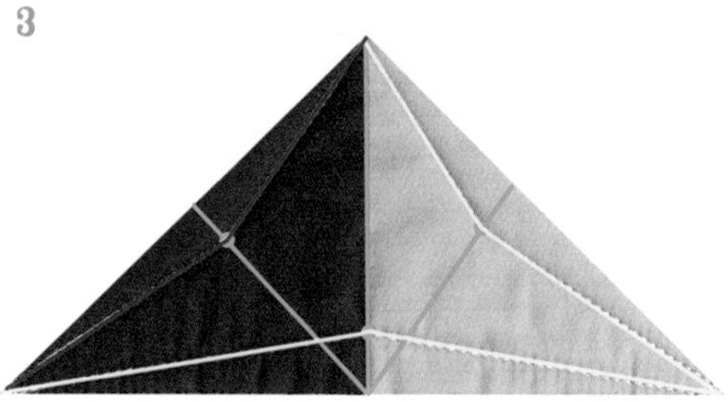

4

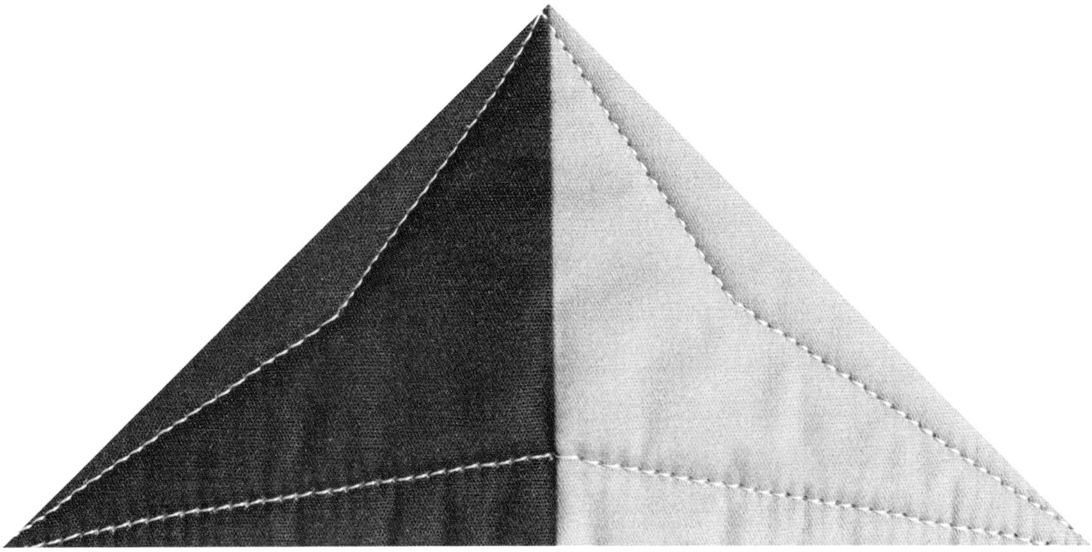

Three-Pointed Star Variation

This variation is similar to the Three-Pointed Star, but this time you'll just make your markings ½″ from the bottom center point, and then stitch just two lines.

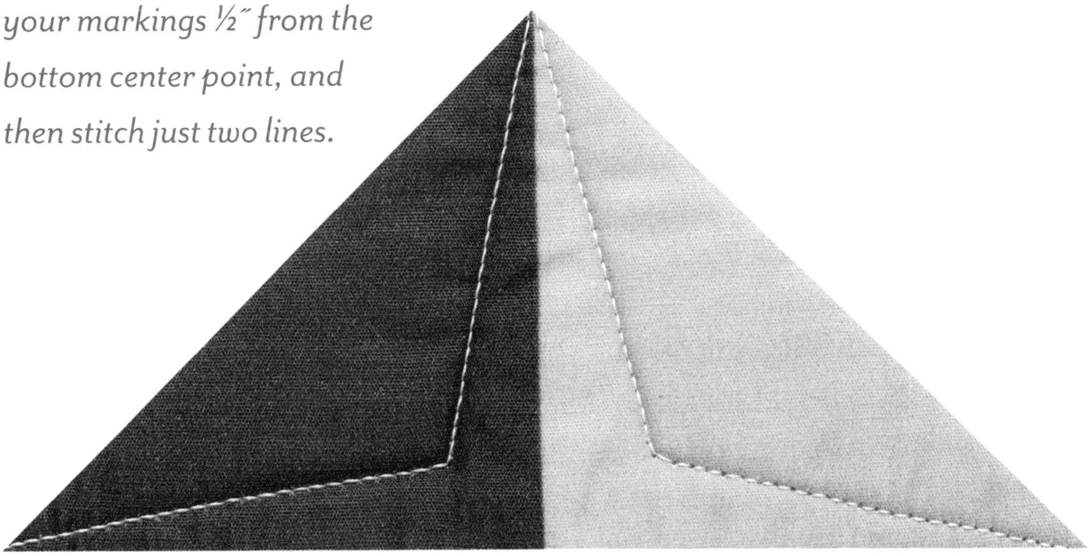

PEAKS

This fun design really creates a lot of interest and can play little tricks on your mind. I recommend drawing out this design before you start stitching, just to avoid any confusion.

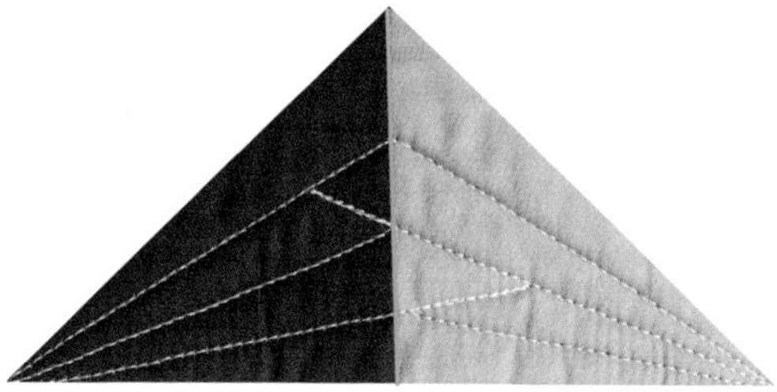

1

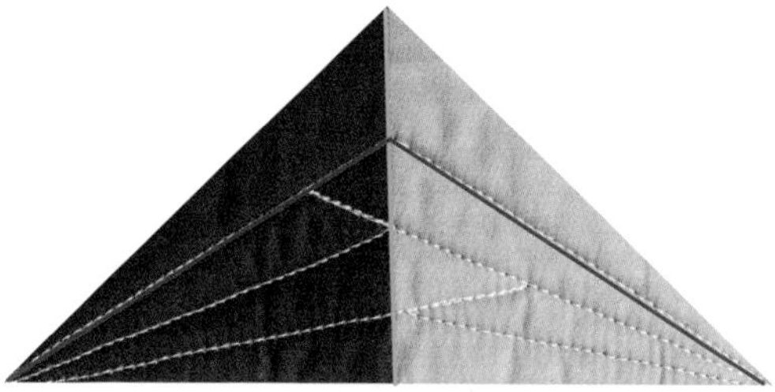

2

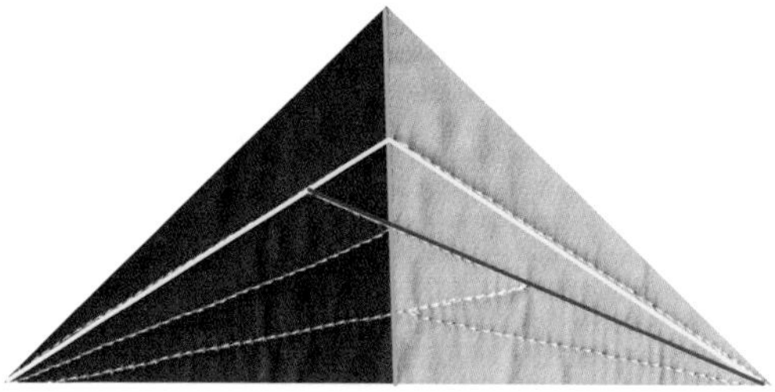

3

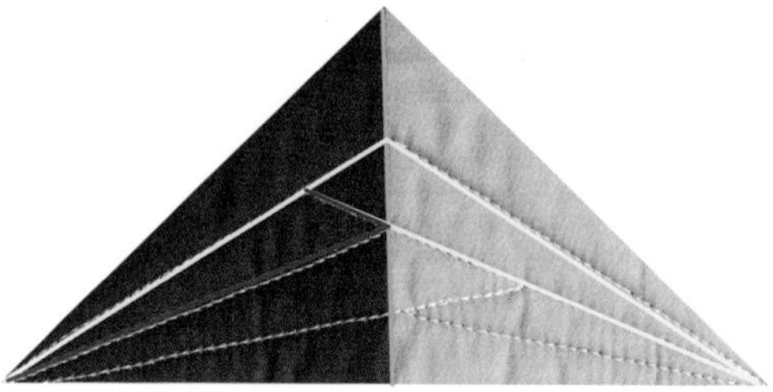

4

STEP 1 • *Draw a straight line through the center of the block using a blue water-soluble pen.*

STEP 2 • *Beginning in the lower left corner, stitch to the straight marked line at a point ½˝ from the top. Turn and stitch to the lower right corner. Use the markings on your machine quilting ruler to measure, or mark the top point in advance.*

STEP 3 • *From the lower right corner, stitch a straight line to the opposite angular line, crossing over the marked center line and stopping at the stitch line ½˝ from the top stitching point.*

STEP 4 • *Stitch back along the previous stitch line to the blue marked line. From that point, stitch an angular line to the bottom left corner.*

STEP 5 • *From the lower left corner, stitch a straight line to the opposite angular line, crossing over the marked line and stopping ½″ from the previous stitching point.*

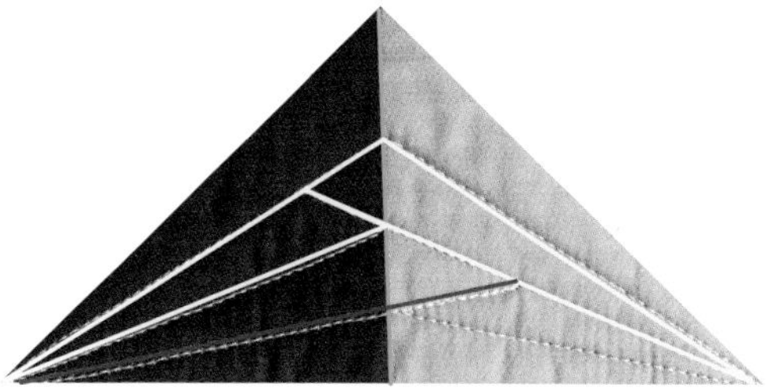

5

> ★ *Natalia's Tip*
>
> I'm not a perfectionist. I love my quilting to look really great, but my spacing does vary slightly. I'm not going to worry about it.

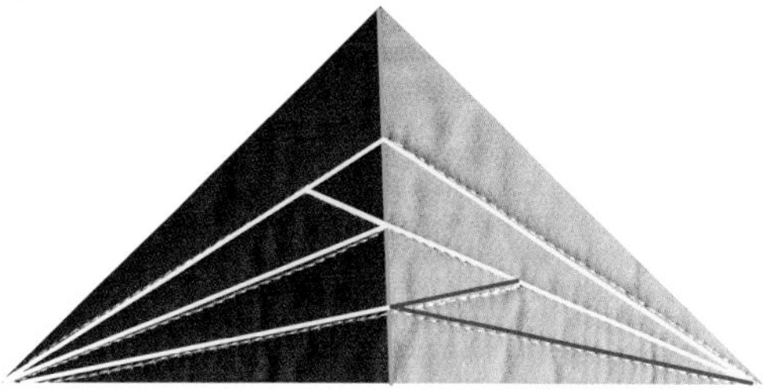

6

STEP 6 • *Stitch back along the previous stitch line to the blue marked line. From there, stitch an angular line to the bottom right corner.*

> ★ *Natalia's Tip*
>
> If the block is a larger block, repeat the pattern until you've filled in the block completely.

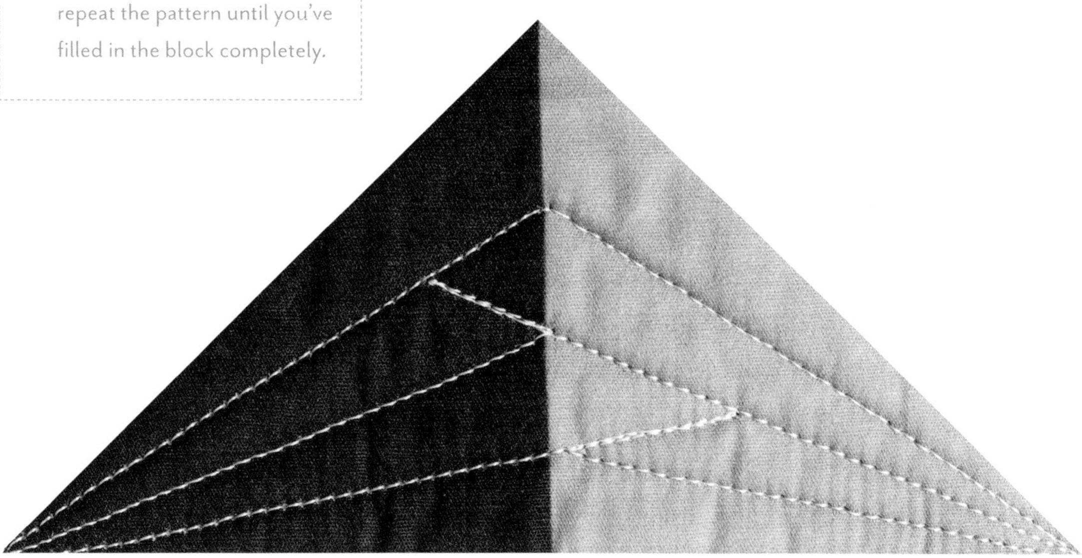

CONTRADICTORY

This fun design is simple, but the stark contrast between the echo line around the top of the triangle and the straight lines creates some fabulous interest, with a place for your eye to rest.

STEP 1 • *Use the straight side of your machine quilting ruler to stitch a straight line ¼″ from the edge of the block, beginning at the lower left corner, to the top center and then to the lower right.*

STEP 2 • *From the lower right corner, stitch-in-the-ditch along the bottom edge to the lower left corner, stopping about ¼″ from the previous stitch line. Turn the ruler and stitch a straight perpendicular line from the bottom of the block to the top angular line.*

STEP 3 • *Stitching along the previous stitch line, travel to the right about ¼″. Use the side of the machine quilting ruler as your guide. Stitch a second parallel line straight down toward the bottom of the block.*

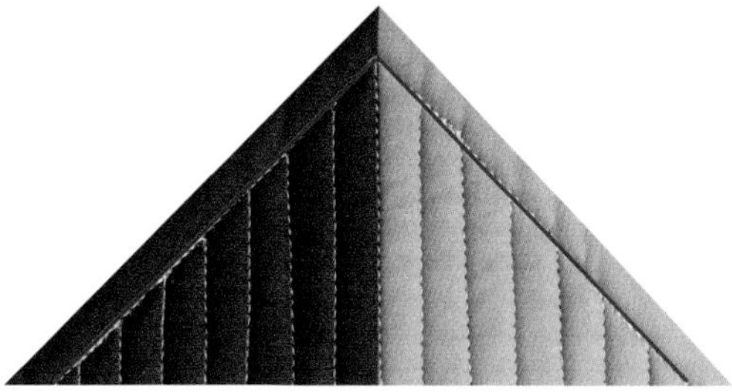

1

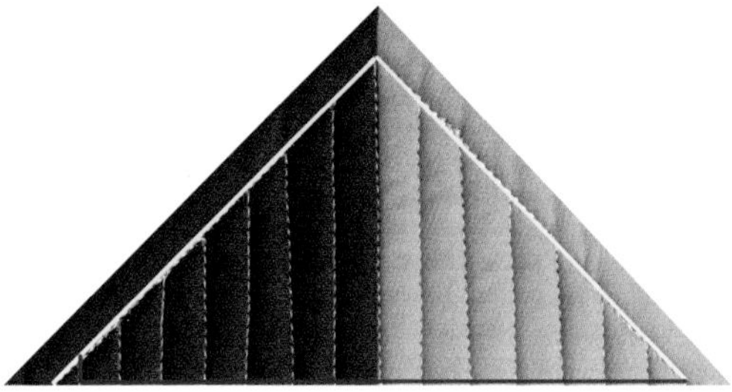

2

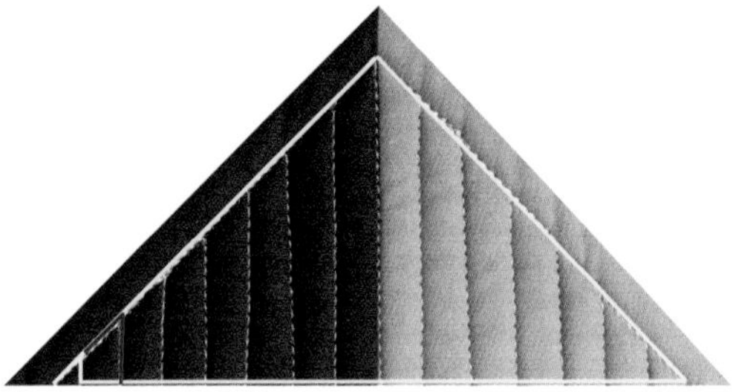

3

STEP 4 · *Stitch-in-the-ditch along the bottom of the block to travel over about ¼″, then turn and stitch a third parallel line to the top stitched line. From that point continue the previous steps, filling in the triangle completely with parallel straight lines.*

STEP 5 · *Stitch-in-the-ditch all the way around the block.*

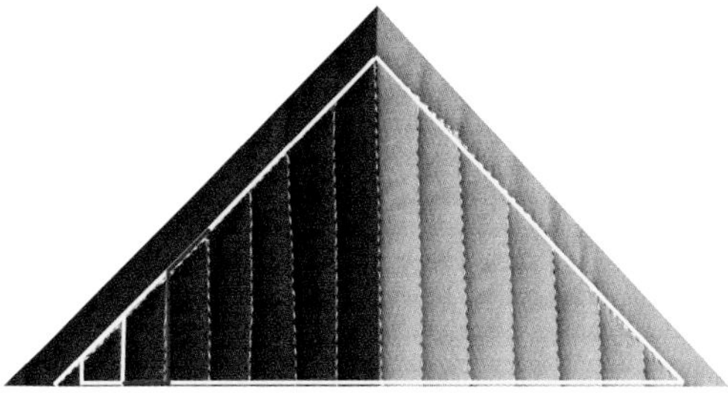

4

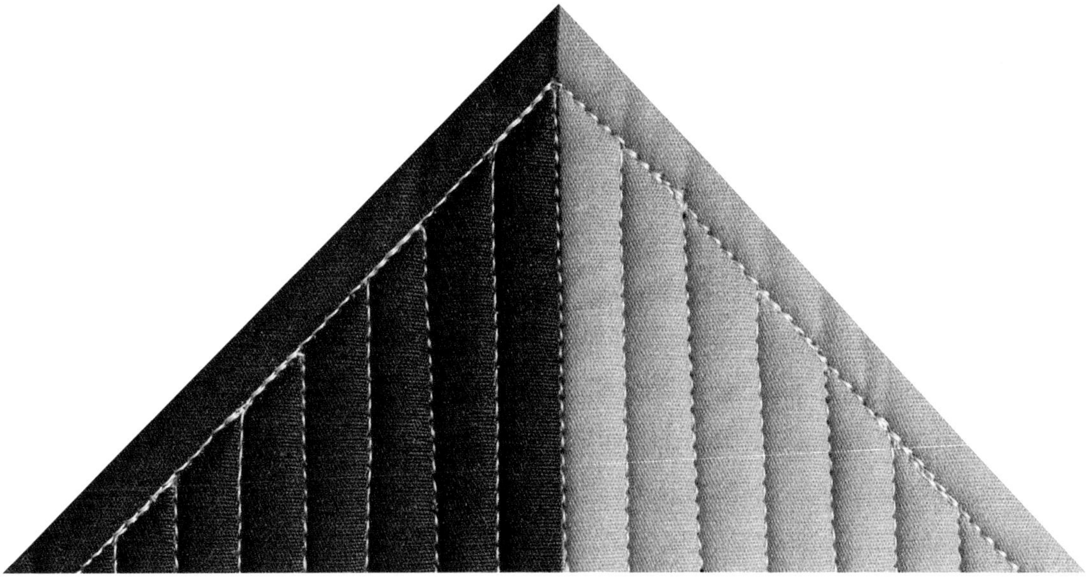

5

CROSSHATCHING

This fun traditional design can be completely stitched out using a machine quilting ruler and no marking.

STEP 1 • *Starting ½˝ from the bottom left corner, use a machine quilting ruler to stitch a parallel line ½˝ from the left side.*

STEP 2 • *From the upper right, stitch-in-the-ditch to travel ½˝ along the right side of the block. Use the markings on the machine quilting ruler to stitch a second straight line, parallel to the previous line, to the bottom of the block.*

STEP 3 • *From the lower left point travel ½˝ across the bottom of the block, then stitch a third parallel line to the right side of the block. Repeat the previous steps until you've filled in the block completely with parallel lines ½˝ apart.*

STEP 4 • *From the bottom edge of the block stitch a straight line ½˝ from the right side of the block to the top left side.*

1

2

3

4

STEP 5 • *From the upper left, stitch-in-the-ditch to travel ½˝ along the left side of the block. From that point, use the markings on the machine quilting ruler to stitch a second straight line, parallel to the previous line, to the bottom of the block.*

STEP 6 • *From the lower right point, travel ½˝ across the bottom of the block, then stitch a third parallel line to the upper left side of the block. Repeat the previous steps until you've filled in the block completely with crosshatching.*

5

6

★ *Natalia's Tip*

To add more interest to this fun design, fill in every other diamond with a heavy filler, like pebbles, swirls or matchstick quilting.

DIAMONDS

This fun design is darling stitched out just as shown here. But to create some fabulous detail, stitch some fun fillers inside the diamonds.

STEP 1 • *Use a blue water-soluble pen to mark 4 lines: 1 horizontal through the center and 3 verticals—1 in the left half, 1 in the center, and 1 in the right half. In this example, the seamline is the center vertical.*

STEP 2 • *Beginning at the center bottom point, stitch to the right point where the 2 lines intersect. Hold your ruler on the triangle's outer edge so the straight line stops ¼″ from the edge of the block. From there, stitch to the top point.*

STEP 3 • *From the top point, stitch to the left point where the 2 lines intersect. Hold your ruler on the triangle's outer edge so the straight line stays ¼″ from the edge of the block. From there stitch to the bottom center point.*

STEP 4 • *From the bottom center point, stitch a diagonal line, holding your ruler so the straight line intersects ¼″ from the left marked line. From that point, stitch a straight line to ¼″ from the bottom left corner, then stitch back to the center point.*

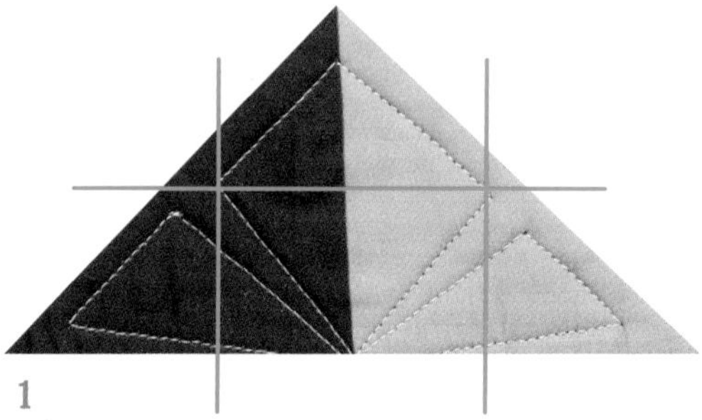

1

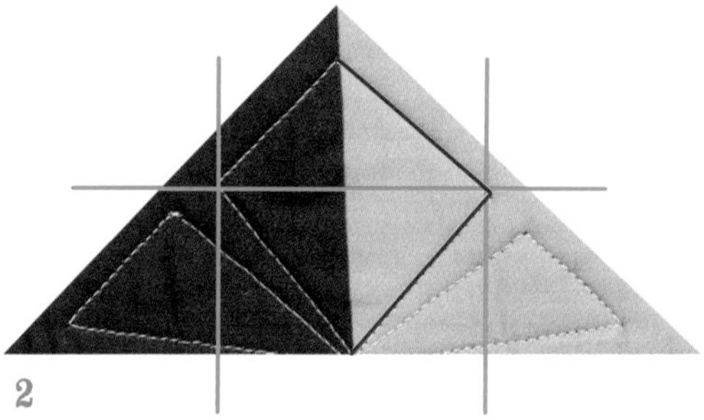

2

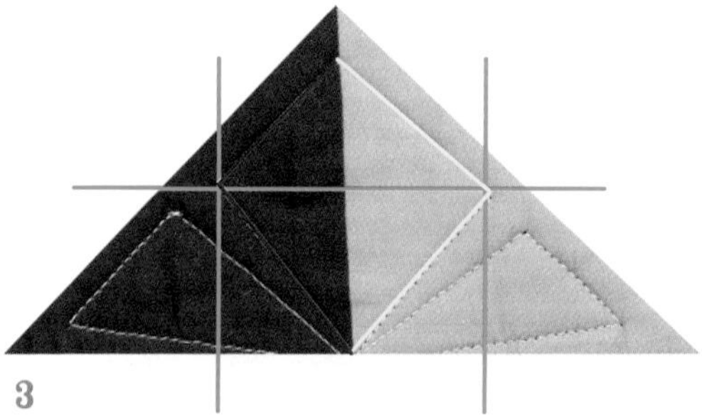

3

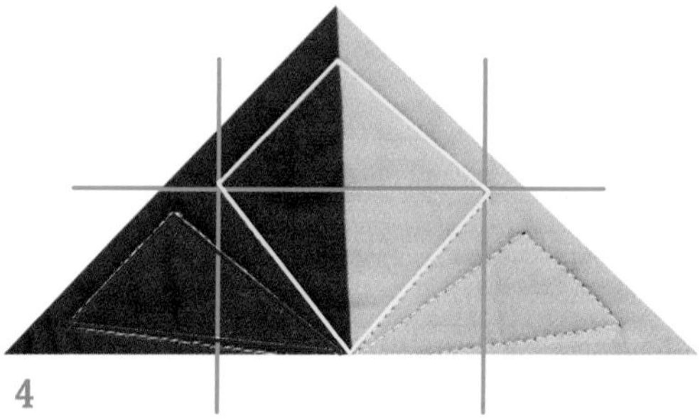

4

STEP 5 • *From the bottom center point, stitch a diagonal line, holding your ruler so the straight line intersects ¼˝ from the right marked line. From that point, stitch a straight line to ¼˝ from the bottom right corner, then stitch back to the center point. From that point stitch-in-the ditch all the way around the block.*

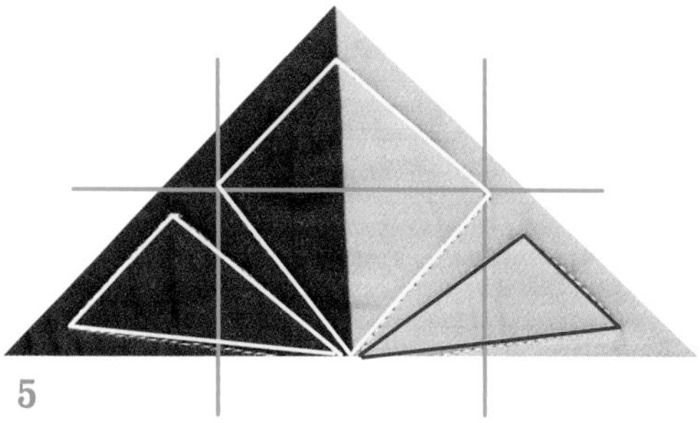

5

BEYOND THE SEAMS

When it comes to modern machine quilting, I love to look at a quilt block and try to extend designs beyond the seams. This design is the perfect example of looking beyond the seams. When you look beyond the seams, secondary designs can start to come to life and your machine quilting can really take off in a creative way.

STEP 1 • *Begin by using a blue water-soluble pen and a ruler to draw a straight line extending from the outside seams. Continue the line until it intersects another block or the edge of the quilt.*

STEP 2 • *Mark a second blue line ¼˝ from the first, also extending it beyond the seams. Continue marking lines until you've filled the desired space completely.*

STEP 3 • *Stitch along the outer marked line, then stitch-in-the-ditch down to the next marked line. Move in the opposite direction to stitch the next line.*

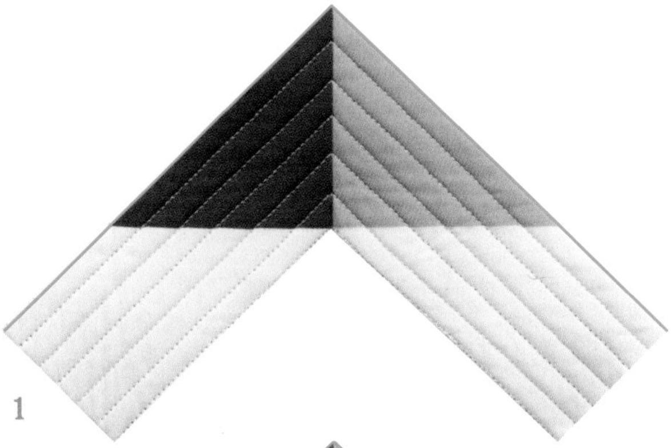

1

2

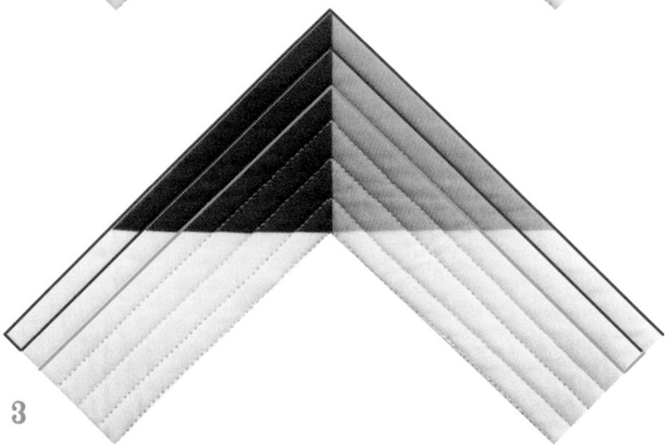

3

STEP 4 • *Continue stitching straight lines until you have filled in the space completely.*

4

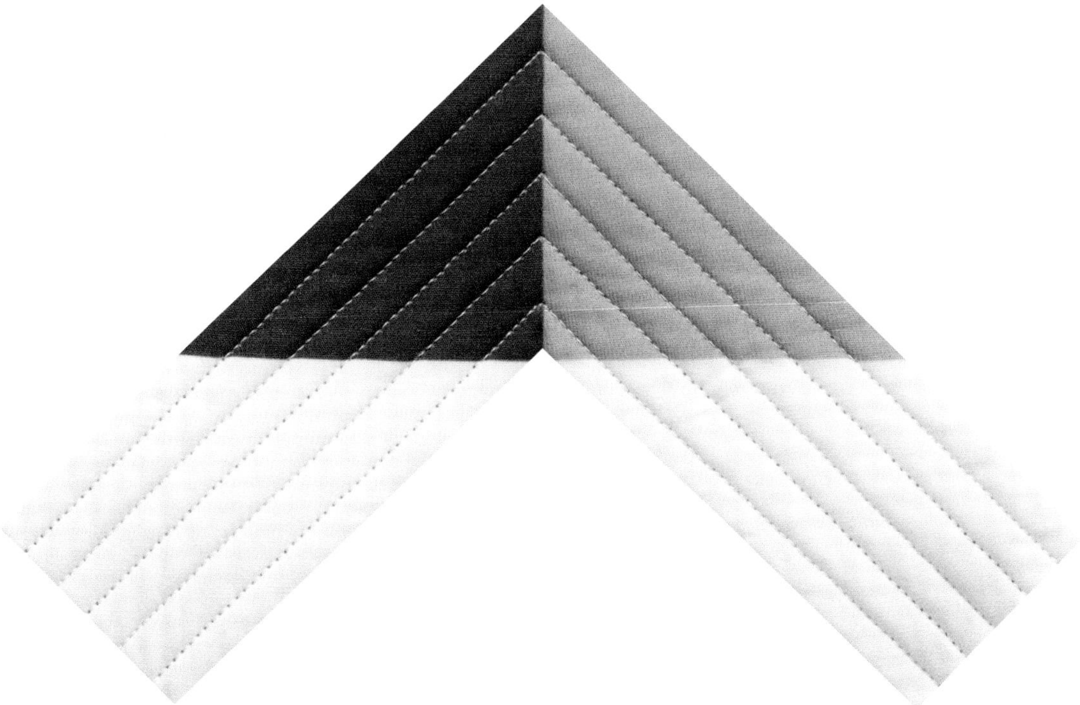

Beyond the Seams Variation

In this variation, I've stitched heavy straight lines between the two lines to create fun texture.

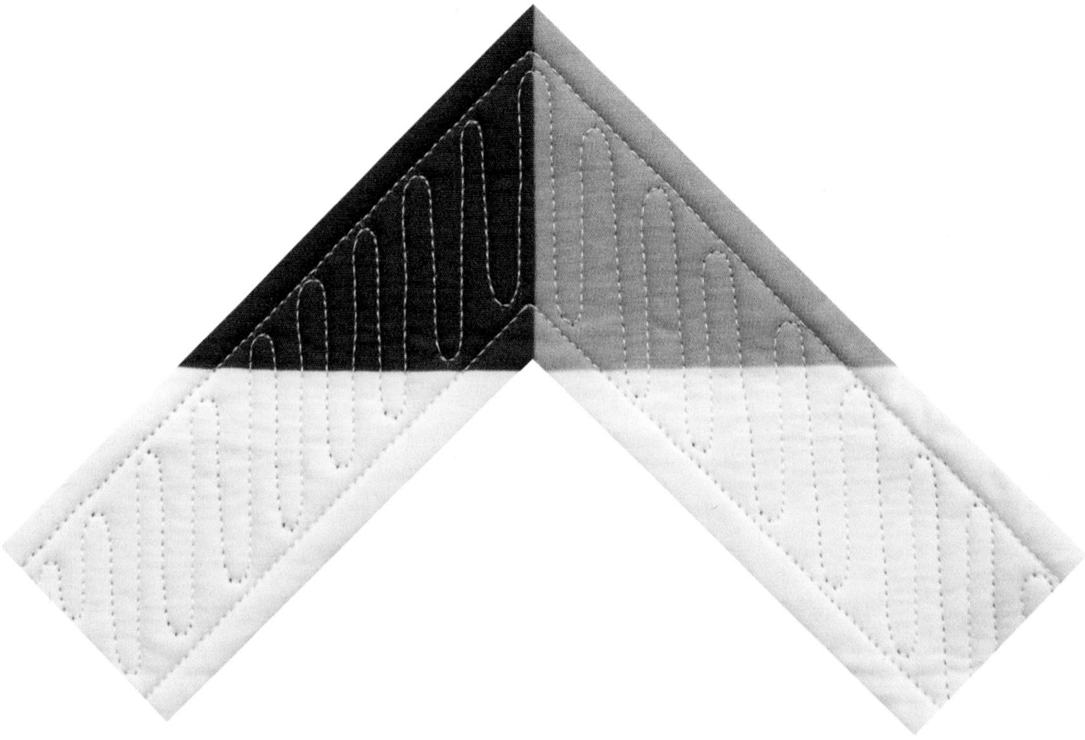

HORIZON

This design is great in a small triangle, like the one shown here, but it could also be beautiful stitched in a large triangle with fun fillers, like matchstick quilting or circles in the large open rows. You could also adjust spacing to fit designs better.

STEP 1 · *Beginning in the bottom left corner, stitch-in-the-ditch all the way around the block. When you get back to the lower left corner, travel ½˝ up the left ditch. From that point, stitch a straight horizontal line ½˝ from the bottom of the block, stopping at the right ditch.*

STEP 2 · *Stitch-in-the-ditch to travel ¼˝ up the right side of the block. Turn and stitch a second horizontal line ¼˝ from the previous line.*

STEP 3 · *Stitch-in-the-ditch to travel ½˝ up the left side of the block. From that point stitch a third horizontal line ½˝ from previous line. From there, stitch-in-the-ditch along the right side of the block and then stitch another horizontal line ¼˝ above that.*

Repeat this process alternating spacing between lines until you've filled in the triangle completely.

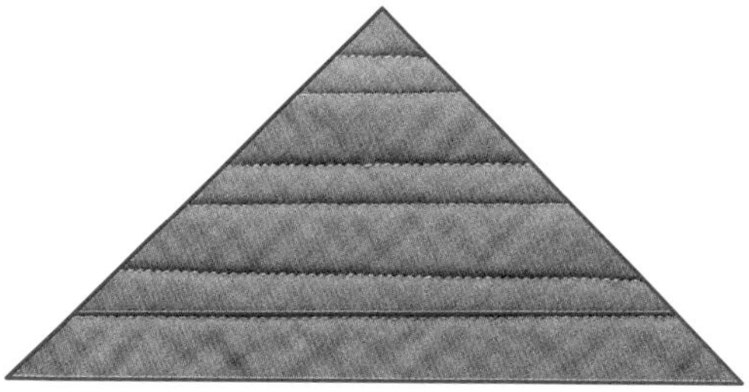

1

2

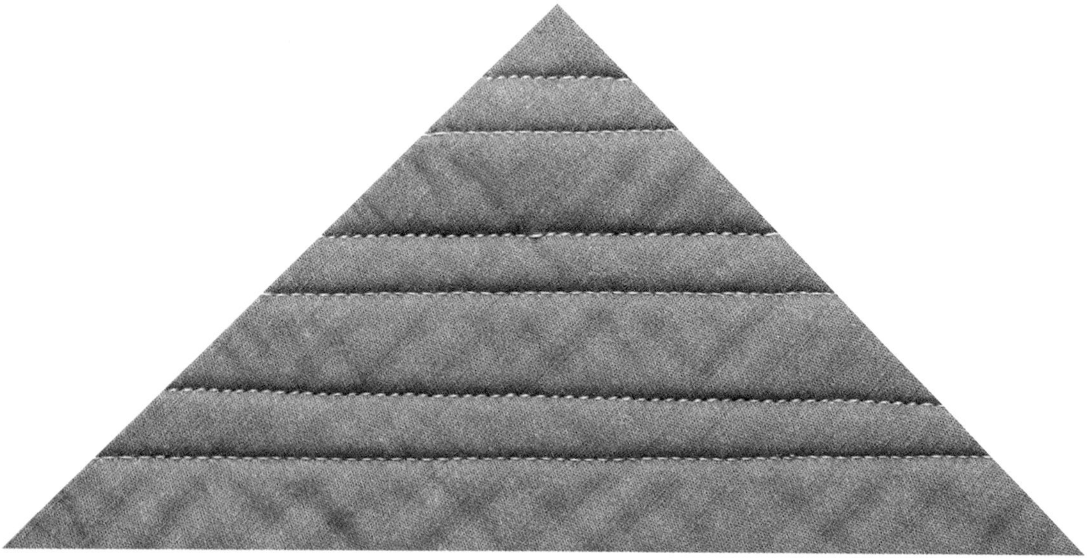

3

ANGULAR TRIANGLE

This fun triangle can be stitched out quite easily, but it's also really cute when four of these triangles are stitched out in a square block. They can create a bit of a rotating look.

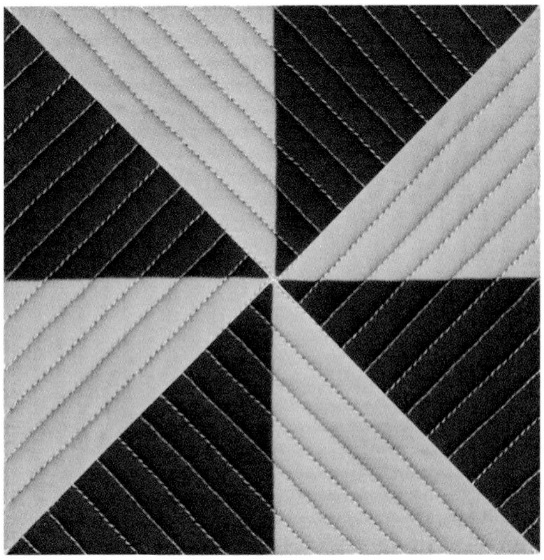

STEP 1 • *Starting at the top of the block, stitch-in-the-ditch all the way around the block. When you get back to the top, travel ½˝ back in-the-ditch toward the left side. From the ½˝ point, stitch a straight line parallel to the right side of the triangle. Use the side of your ruler or a previously marked line to guide you.*

STEP 2 • *Stitch-in-the-ditch ½˝ along the bottom edge, traveling toward the left side of the block. Turn and stitch a second straight line toward the top left side of the block, parallel to the right side of the triangle or previous stitch line.*

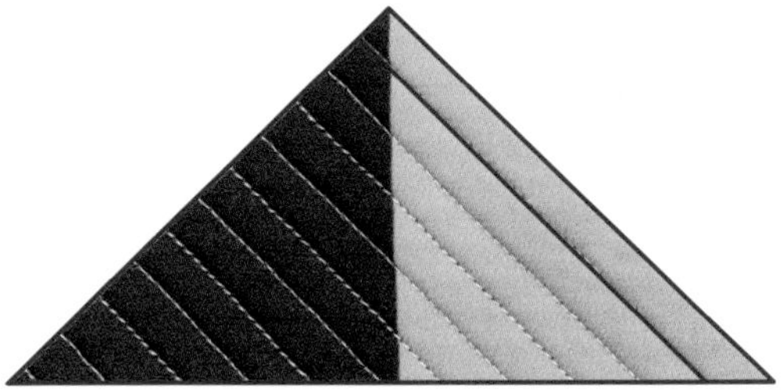

1

2

STEP 3 • *Stitch-in-the-ditch along the top edge of the block moving toward the bottom left ½˝. From that point, turn and stitch a third parallel line. Continue to travel in-the-ditch ½˝ to fill the block with parallel lines.*

★ *Natalia's Tip*

I prefer to space my lines for this design ½˝ apart because I prefer my quilting to be a bit on the heavier side. If you like your quilting a bit looser, consider making your lines ¾˝ to 1˝ apart.

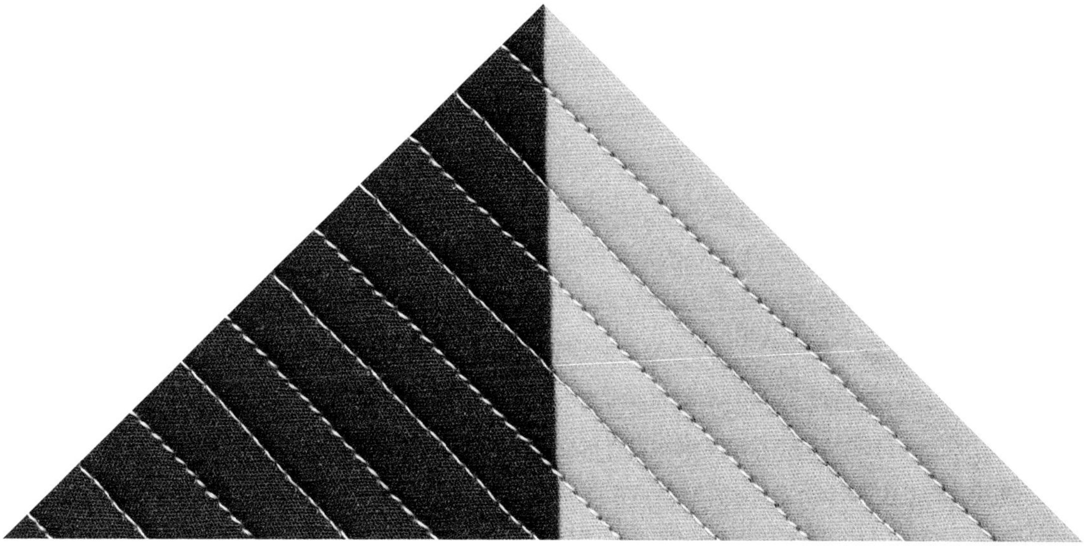

3

TRIPLE TRIANGLE

This design is so cool when it's quilted in a large triangle. It adds a lot of interest and fills in negative space nicely.

STEP 1 • *Begin by finding and marking the center on all three sides of the triangle, Mark a vertical straight line through the center of the block.*

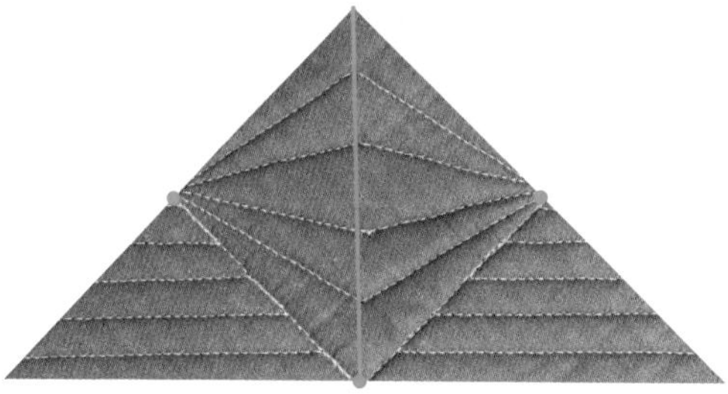

1

★ Natalia's Tip

Before you begin stitching, you could mark reference points ½″ apart along the straight line. If you're using a machine quilting ruler, you can use the measurements on the ruler to measure your spacing. This will eliminate some marking and save a little bit of time.

2

STEP 2 • *Beginning at the marked point on the left side of the triangle, stitch-in-the-ditch all the way around the triangle. When you get back to the starting point, stitch a straight line to the bottom center point, then up to the right center point.*

STEP 3 • *From the right side, stitch a straight line to a point on the center marked line, ½″ from the bottom point. From that point, stitch a straight line to the left marked point.*

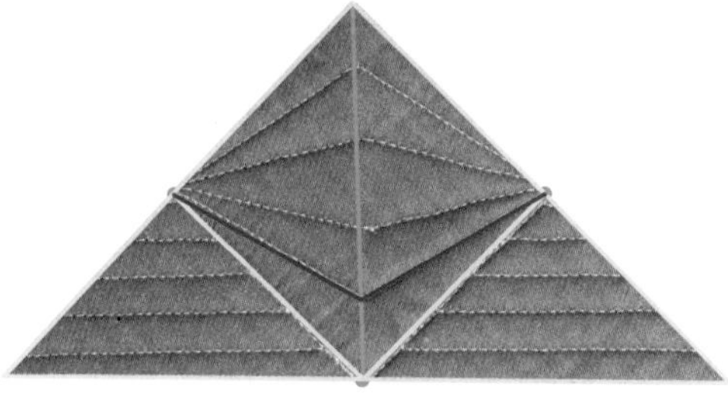

3

STEP 4 • *From the left side, stitch a straight line to the center marked line, this time intersecting the center line ½″ above the previous stitch line. From there, stitch a straight line back to the right side marked point.*

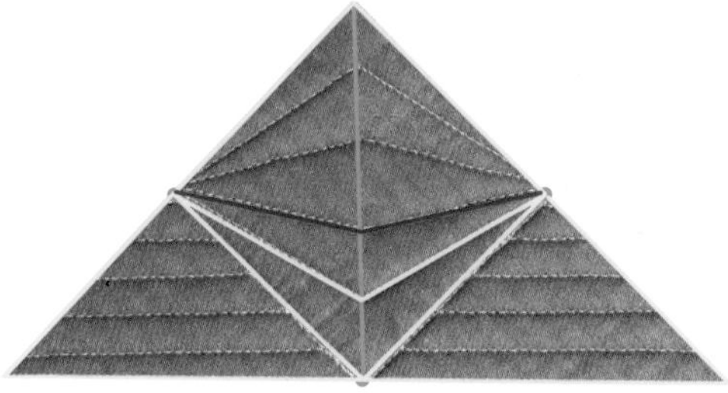

4

STEP 5 • *Repeat Steps 3 and 4 on the top side of the square to finish that section of the block.*

STEP 6 • *From the right marked point, stitch-in-the-ditch down the right side of the block to ½˝ from the bottom point. From that point, stitch a horizontal line parallel to the bottom side of the block.*

STEP 7 • *Stitch ½˝ up along the previous stitching, then stitch a second horizontal line.*

STEP 8 • *Repeat Steps 6 and 7 until you've filled in the right side of the block completely with parallel lines.*

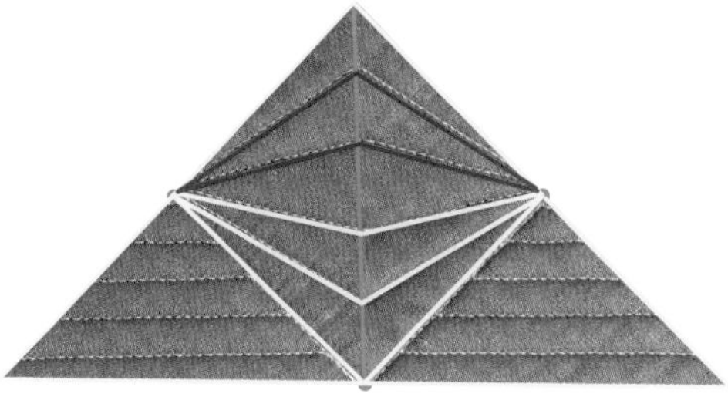

5

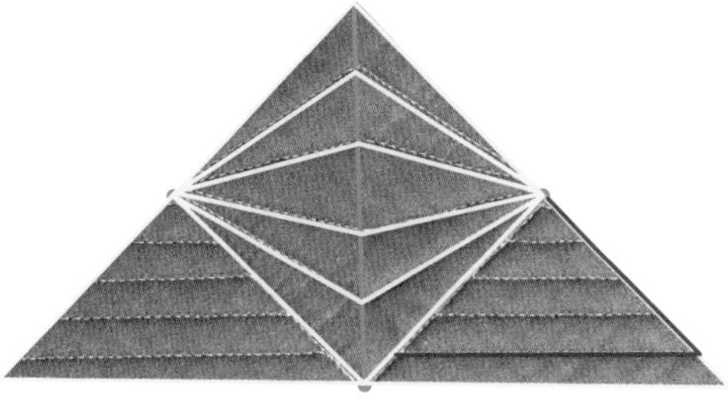

6

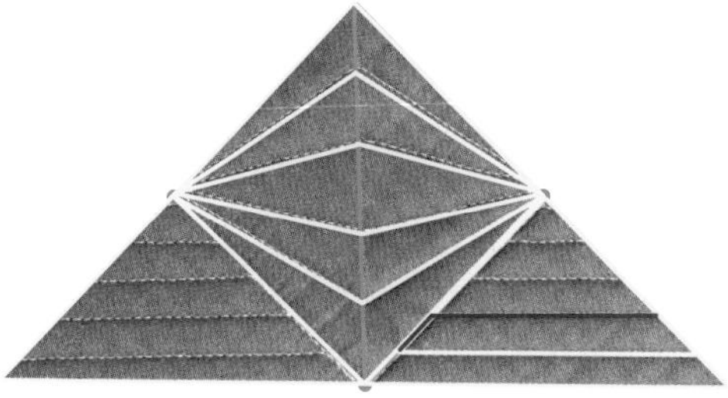

7

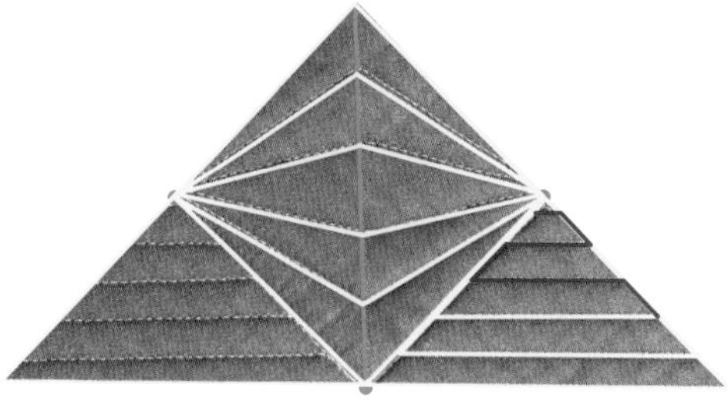

8

STEP 9 • *Stitch-in-the-ditch back down the right side of the block and along the bottom until you reach the left triangle. Follow the previous steps to stitch the same design on the left side.*

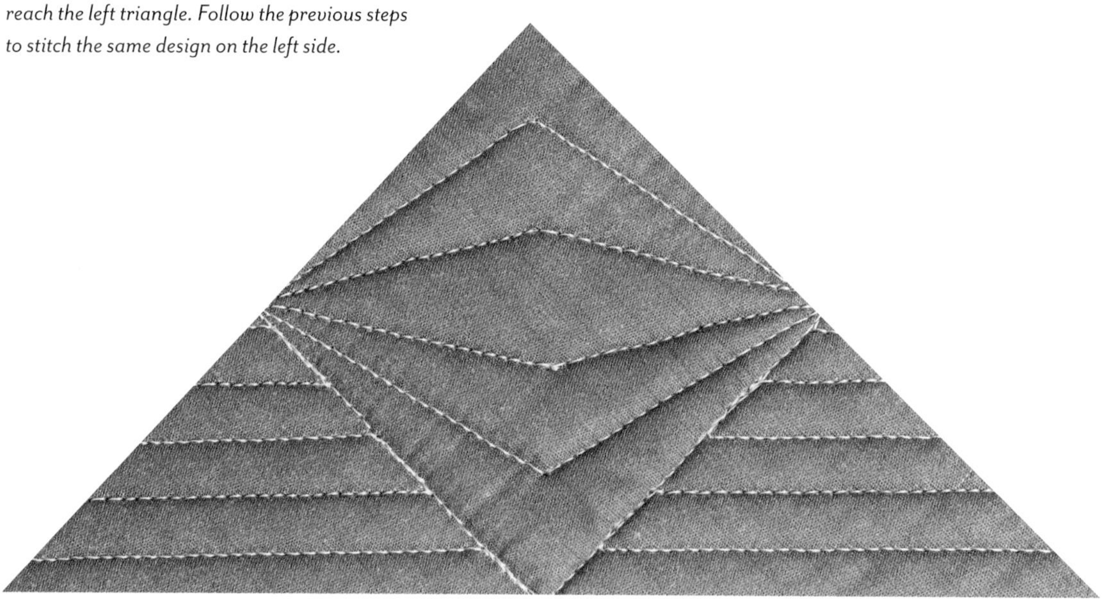

9

SIMPLE TRIANGLE

Quilt blocks don't always need heavy quilting, and this block is the perfect example of that. This block is a pieced triangle, but it'd also look great on a solid triangle.

1

2

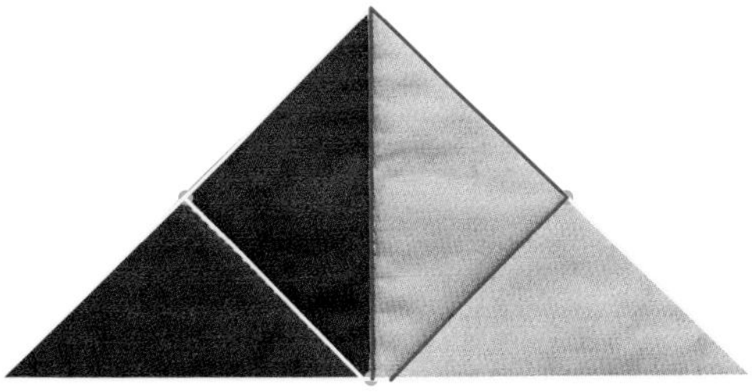

3

STEP 1 • *Mark the center point on all 3 sides of the triangle.*

STEP 2 • *Beginning at the left marked point, stitch-in-the-ditch all the way around the block. When you get back to the left point, stitch a straight line to the bottom center point on the block.*

STEP 3 • *From the bottom center point, stitch a straight line to the top center point on the block. From there, stitch-in-the-ditch to the marked point on the right side of the block. From that point, stitch a straight line to the bottom center point.*

INSIDE TRIANGLES

This design is great for any, more modern triangle. To dress up this design, quilt small circles in every other one of the rows that are created with your quilting.

STEP 1 • *Mark a straight line through the center of the triangle.*

> ★ *Natalia's Tip*
>
> At this point you could also mark points along the centerline every ½″ apart.

STEP 2 • *Beginning in the lower left corner, stitch-in-the-ditch all the way around the block. When you reach the bottom left corner, travel ½″ back along the previous stitch line.*

STEP 3 • *From that point stitch a line parallel to the left side of the triangle all the way to the marked centerline. Turn and stitch a line parallel on the right side of the block.*

STEP 4 • *Stitch ½″ in-the-ditch along the bottom of the block. Stitch another line parallel to the first, turning at the center line ½″ from the first marked point.*

1

2

3

4

STEP 5 • *Repeat Steps 3 and 4 until you've filled in the block completely with straight lines ½″ apart.*

5

Inside Triangles Variation

In this variation, I've quilted the straight lines the opposite direction of the triangle to create more interest. Simple changes make big impact.

DOUBLE BURST

This design adds a little bit of texture to a plain triangle. This design is great if it's measured out and quilted very precisely, but it can also be fun a little more improv.

STEP 1 • *Mark a vertical straight line down the center of the triangle.*

STEP 2 • *Beginning at the bottom center point of the triangle, stitch-in-the-ditch all the way around the block.*

STEP 3 • *When you return to the center point, stitch a straight line toward the left side of the block, stopping ¼˝ from the bottom and ¼˝ from the left side of the block.*

STEP 4 • *Stitch a line parallel to the left side of the block, ¼˝ from the left side of the block stopping ¼˝ from the top of the block. From that point, stitch a straight line back to the center point.*

STEP 5 • *From the center point, repeat the shape in Step 3 by stitching to points ¼˝ from the previous stitch line, then back to the bottom point.*

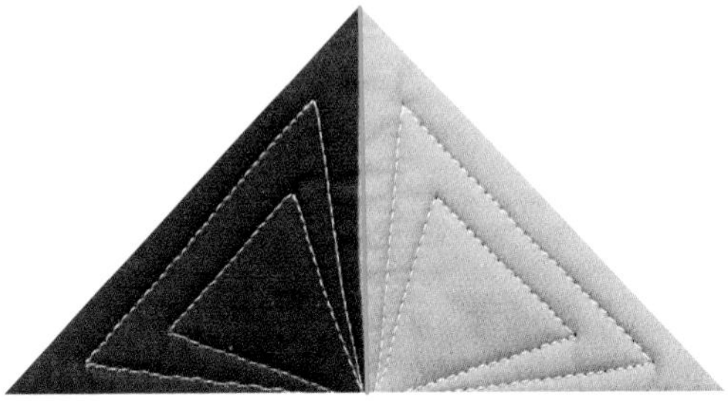

1

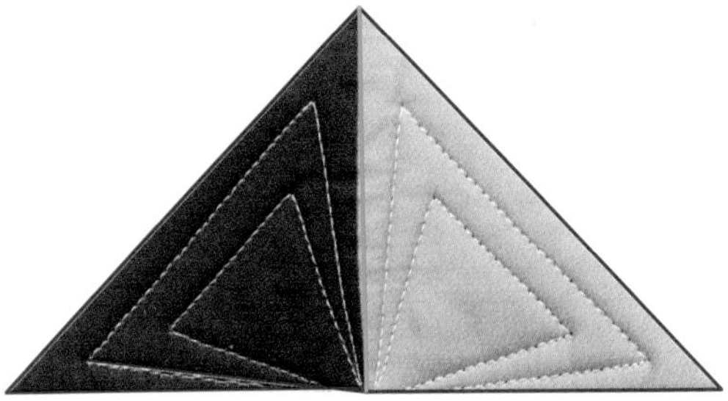

2 & 3

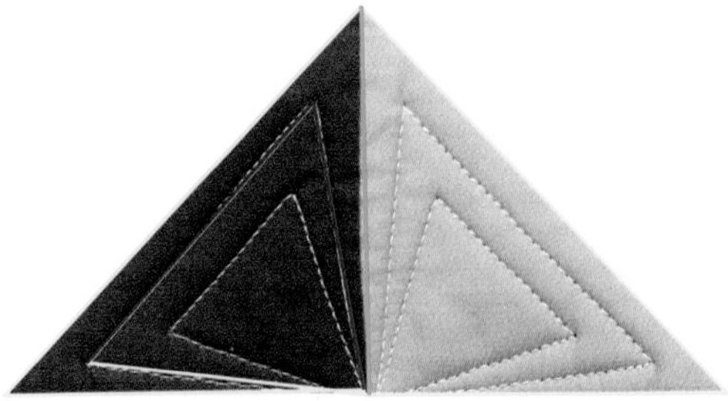

4

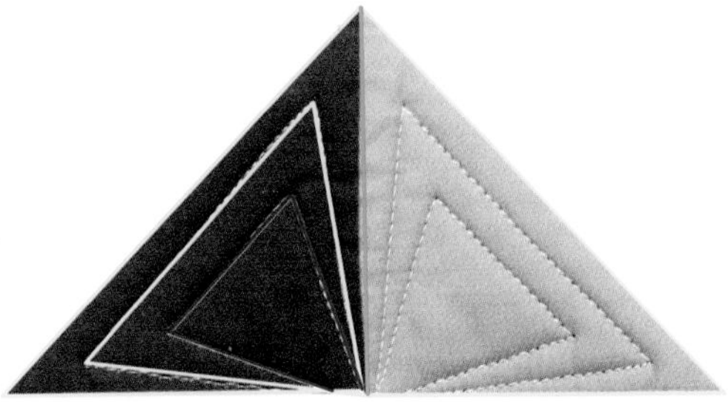

5

STEP 6 • *When you return to the center point, repeat Steps 3–5 to fill in the right side of the block.*

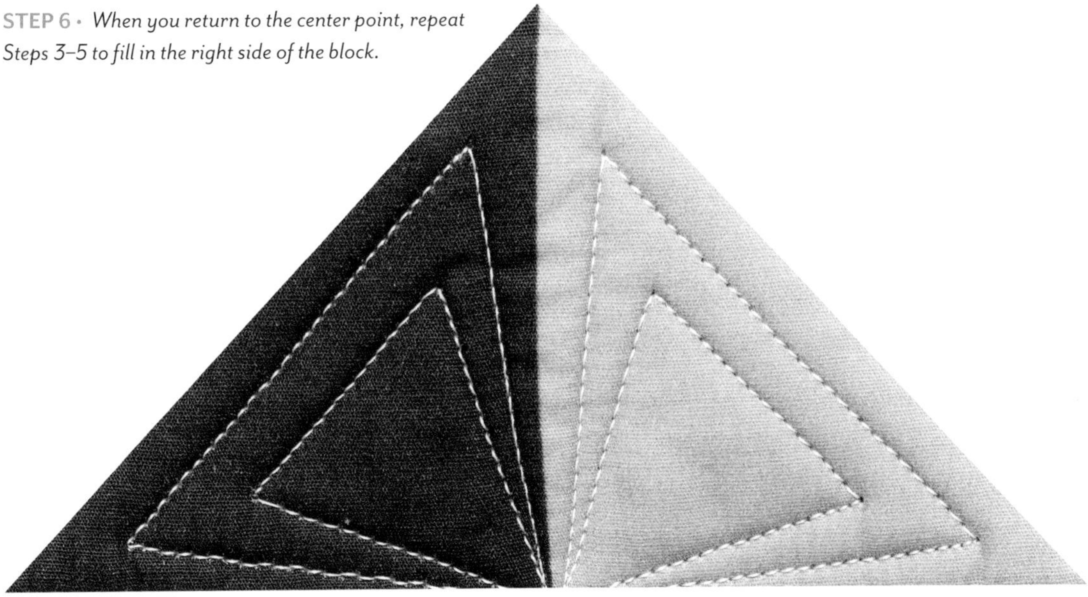

6

Double Burst Variation

In this variation design, I stitched a straight line through the vertical center of the block and then stitched only one inside echo.

SUNRAYS

This design can add so much texture to a quilt. It would be really cute quilted to look like the rays of sunshine or it could even resemble a snowflake.

STEP 1 • *Find the center point along the bottom edge of the block. Starting there, stitch-in-the-ditch all the way around the block. When you get back to the center, stitch a straight line toward a point that is ¼″ from the bottom and left edge of the triangle. From that point, stitch on the previous stitch line back to the center of the block.*

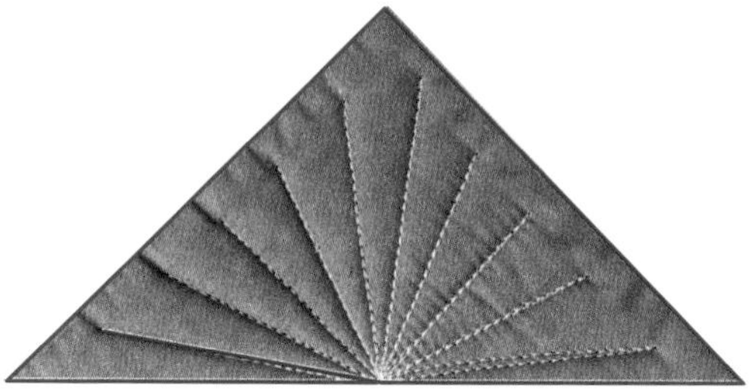

1

★ Natalia's Tip

If you're using a ruler foot, stop stitching when the side of the foot reaches the outside of the block. This will eliminate the need for extra marking or measuring.

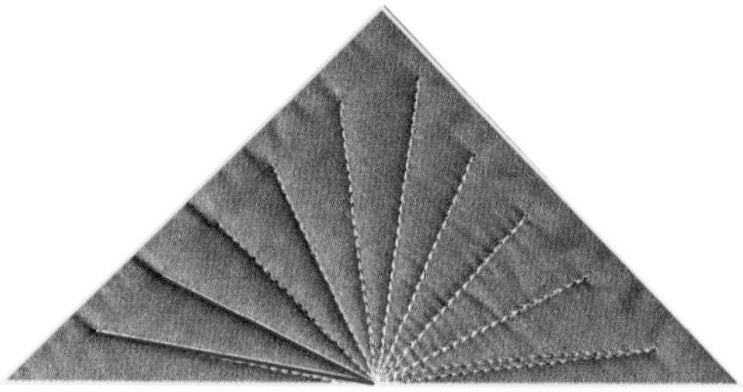

2

STEP 2 • *From the center point, stitch a straight line toward a point that is ¼″ from the first point. Stitch on the previous stitch line back to the center of the block.*

STEP 3 • *Repeat Step 2 to continue filling in the block.*

3

TOP RAY

This design is an interesting way to make your quilt block look a little bit taller than it actually is.

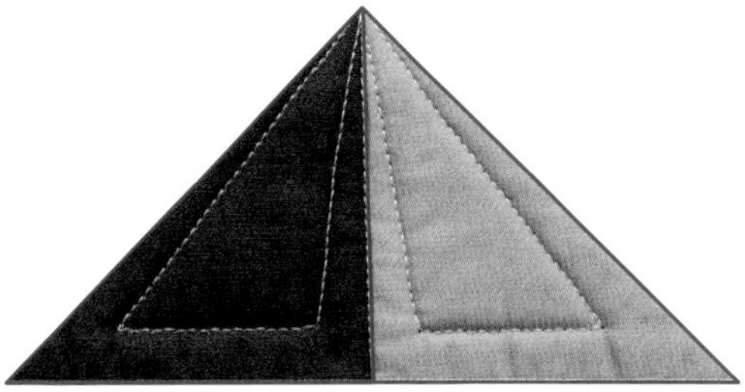

1

STEP 1 • *Beginning at the bottom center point of the triangle, stitch-in-the-ditch all the way around the block. When you return to the center point, stitch a straight vertical line up through the center of the block.*

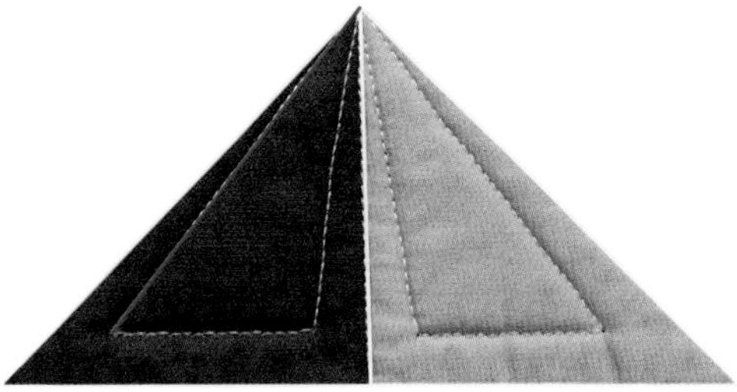

2

STEP 2 • *From the top center point, stitch a straight line toward the bottom left side of the block, stopping ¼″ from the bottom and left sides of the block.*

3

STEP 3 • *From that point, stitch a straight line parallel to the bottom of the triangle, stopping ¼″ from the center line. From that point, stitch a straight line back to the top of the block.*

STEP 4 • *Repeat Steps 2 and 3 to stitch the same design on the right side of the block.*

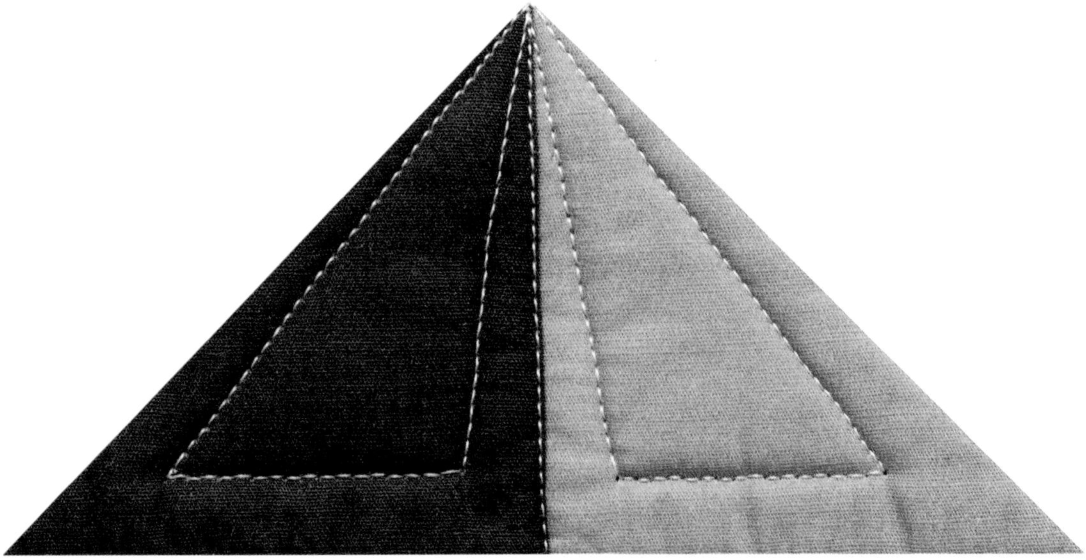

4

ANGLE MAZE

This design can be stitched in a small triangle or a large triangle. Simply adjust the spacing to make it fit accordingly.

STEP 1 • *Beginning in the lower right corner, stitch-in-the-ditch all the way around the block. When you get back to the lower right corner, travel ¼˝ in-the-ditch along the bottom of the block. From that point, stitch a line parallel to the right side of the block stopping ¼˝ from the top of the block.*

STEP 2 • *Turn and stitch a line ¼˝ long, parallel to the top left side of the block. From that point, turn and stitch a line parallel to the first stitched line, stopping ¼˝ from the bottom edge of the block.*

STEP 3 • *Turn and stitch another ¼˝ line parallel to the bottom edge of the block, then turn and stitch another straight line parallel to the right side of the block. From that point, stitch a ¼˝ straight line parallel to the left side of the block.*

1

2

3

STEP 4 · *Repeat Steps 2 and 3 until you've filled in the block completely. When you get to the left side of the block, stitch an angled line to the bottom left corner.*

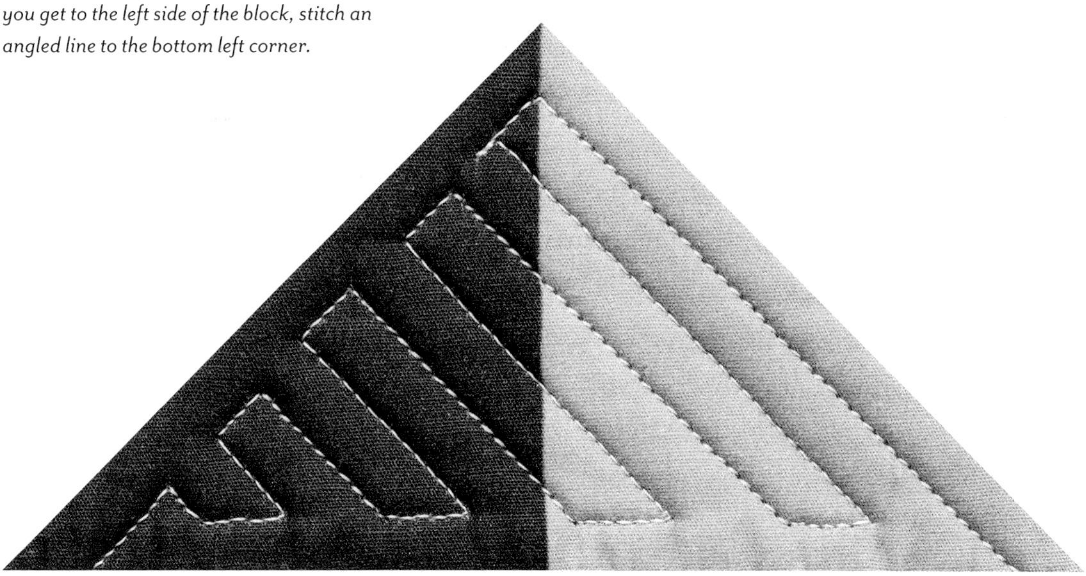

4

TRIANGLE SPIRAL

This design is great for modern-type quilting. While it is shown here on a pieced triangle, it also would work well on an unpieced block.

STEP 1 • *Beginning in the lower left corner, stitch-in-the-ditch all the way around the block. Stitch ¼˝ up the left ditch. From that point, stitch a straight line parallel to the bottom of the block, stopping ¼˝ from the right side of the triangle.*

STEP 2 • *Turn and stitch a straight line parallel to the right side of the triangle, stopping ¼˝ from the top left side of the block.*

STEP 3 • *Turn and stitch a straight line parallel to the left side of the block, stopping ¼˝ from the previous stitch line. From that point, turn and stitch another straight line parallel to the bottom of the triangle, stopping ¼˝ from the stitched line.*

1

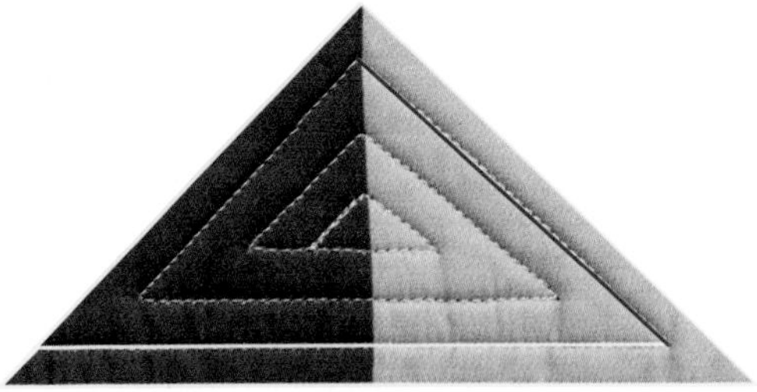

2

3

STEP 4 · *Continue stitching straight lines ¼˝ apart, spiraling toward the center of the block. When you reach a point that you can no longer stitch straight lines, stitch into the previous stitch line and tie off the threads.*

4

Square BLOCK DESIGNS

All designs in this section are for a single block. To create more interest in your machine quilting, combine a few designs throughout the quilt. Or simply repeat the same design but alternate the orientation to help bring secondary designs to life.

SQUARE FLOWER

This design is a nice way to add a flower into a more modern quilt. I love stitching out this design because you do not need to be perfect to make it work.

STEP 1 • *Beginning at the upper right center of the block, stitch a straight line toward the right edge, stopping ¼˝ from the edge. From there stitch a straight line, parallel to the right side of the block, traveling any distance from ½˝ to 1˝. From there, turn and stitch a straight line back to the starting point.*

STEP 2 • *From the center point, stitch a second petal by following the same process as in Step 1.*

STEP 3 • *Repeat Step 2 until you've completely filled the block with petals. When you come to a corner, to create a little more interest you can even turn around the corner.*

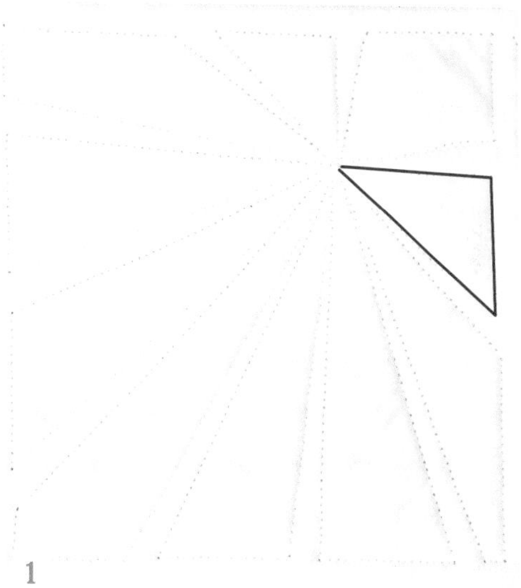

1

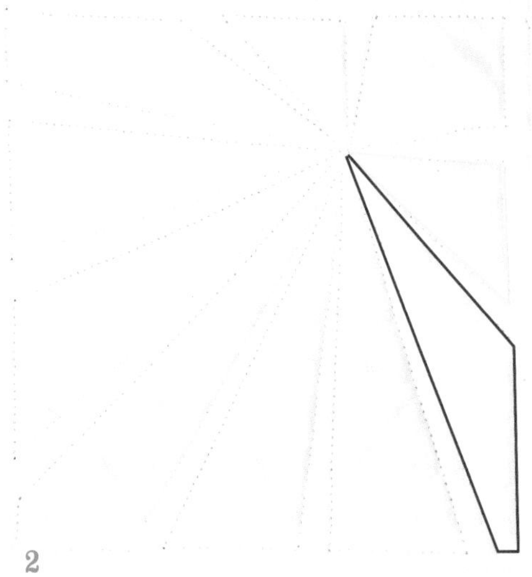

2

PERPENDICULAR LINES

The Perpendicular Lines design looks great on a single block. But if you quilted it in each quarter of a four-block design, rotating the orientation, you'd create an awesome diamond design in the center.

STEP 1 • *Beginning in the lower left corner, stitch a diagonal line from the bottom left to the upper right.*

STEP 2 • *From the upper right corner, travel over the top ditch about ½″. From that point, use the first marking on your machine quilting ruler (½″) to stitch a second line, parallel to the first line, from the upper right to the lower left.*

★ *Natalia's Tip*

If you want to use your walking foot to stitch this design, Premark the lines ½″ apart.

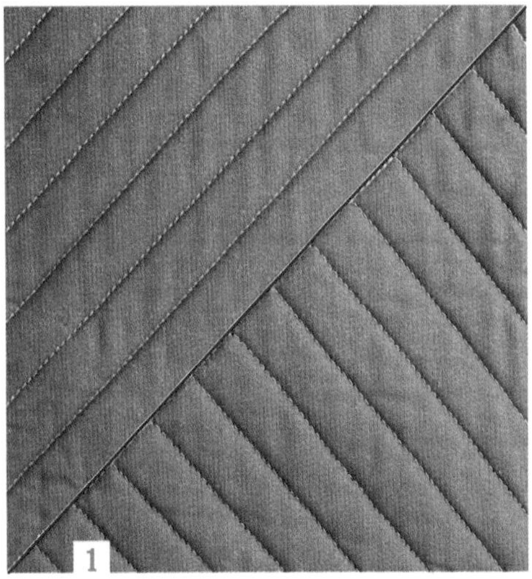

1

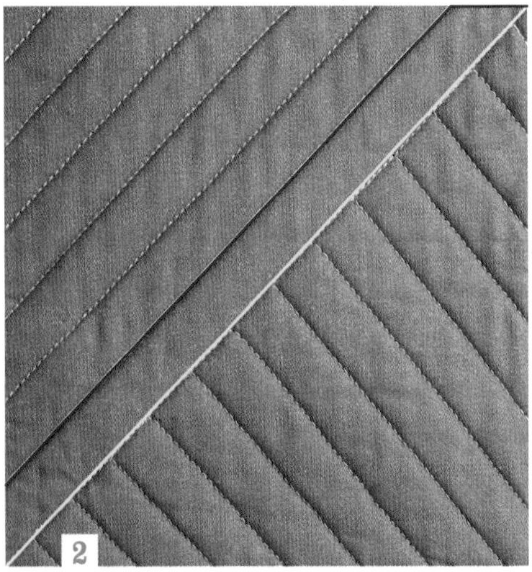

2

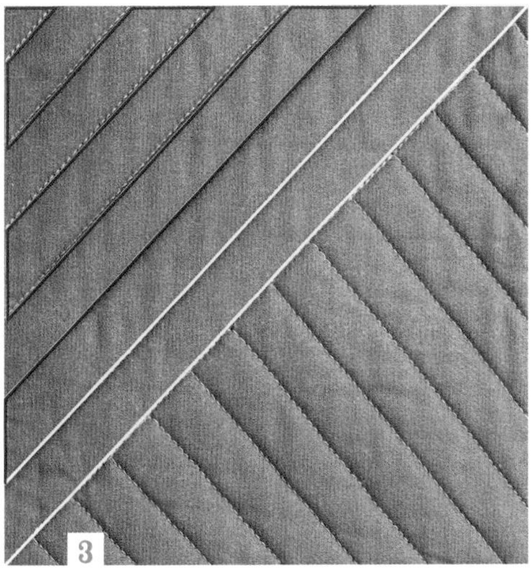

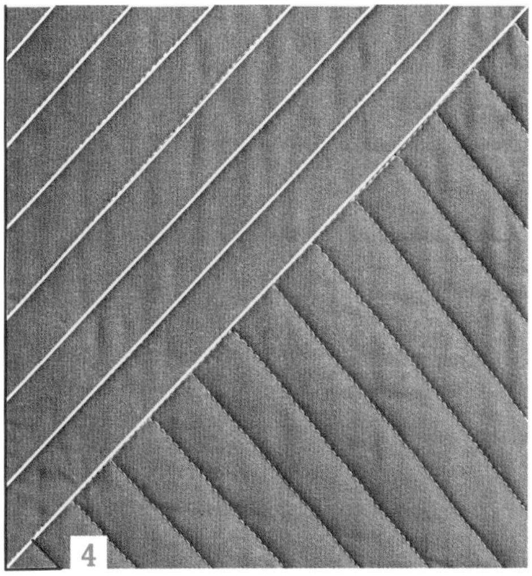

STEP 3 • *From that point, travel ½˝ up the left ditch. Use the first marking on your machine quilting ruler to stitch another line parallel to the previous lines. Repeat the previous steps until you've filled in the top left half of the block with parallel lines.*

STEP 4 • *Stitch-in-the-ditch along the left side of the block to the bottom corner, then travel ½˝ along the bottom. At that point, turn and stitch a straight line, perpendicular to the previous lines. Stop at the center diagonal line.*

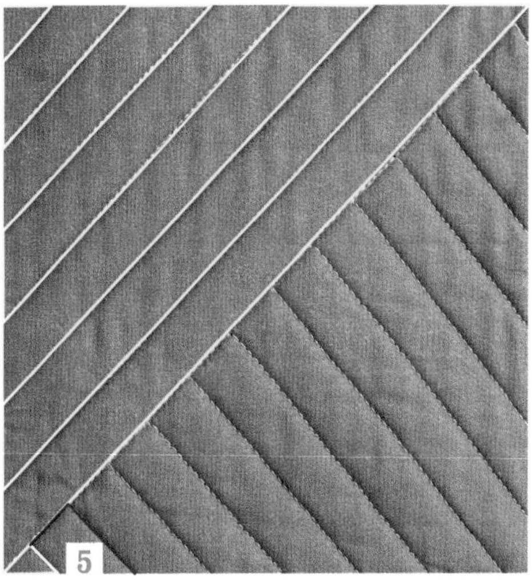

STEP 5 • *Stitch along the center stitch line about ½˝, then turn and stitch a straight line to the bottom of the block, parallel to the previous stitch line. Continue the pattern until you fill in the bottom right side of the block with straight lines perpendicular to the top half of the block.*

Stitch-in-the-ditch all the way around the block.

LOCKED IN

In the sample, I've used a machine quilting ruler, but this could be done free-motion with no ruler to have a little bit more organic look.

STEP 1 • *Beginning in the upper left corner, stitch-in-the-ditch all the way around the block. When you get back to the upper left corner, stitch-in-the-ditch again about ¼˝ to the right. Then stitch a straight line toward the bottom of the block along the left side, stopping about ¼˝ from the bottom edge.*

STEP 2 • *From that point, turn and stitch a straight line parallel to the bottom edge. Stop ¼˝ from the right side.*

STEP 3 • *Turn and stitch a straight line parallel to the right side, stopping ¼˝ from the top.*

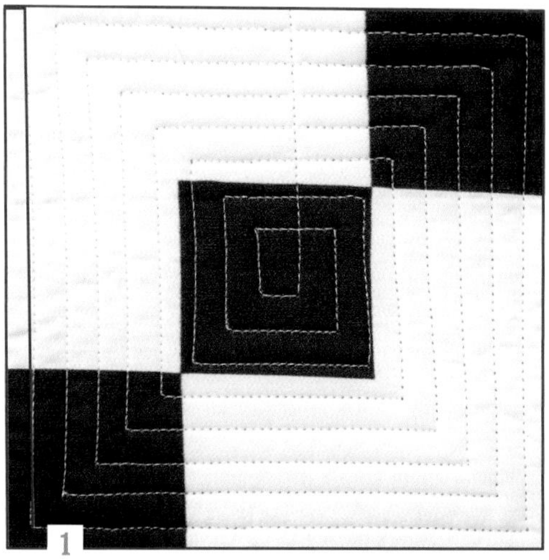

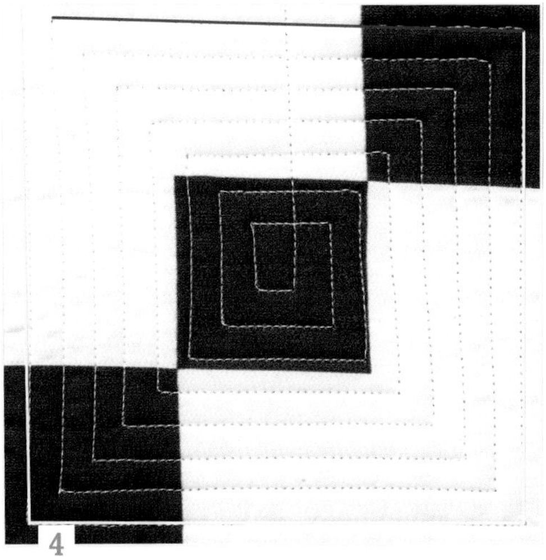

STEP 4 • *Turn and stitch a straight line parallel to the top, stopping ¼˝ from the previous stitch line.*

STEP 5 • *Repeat the previous steps, stitching a square spiral all the way to the inside of the block. Keep your stitching lines about ¼˝ apart.*

★ *Natalia's Tip*

If you like looser quilting, stitch your lines about ½˝ apart.

STEP 6 • *Once you've reached the center of the block stitch a straight line out from the center to the edge of the block.*

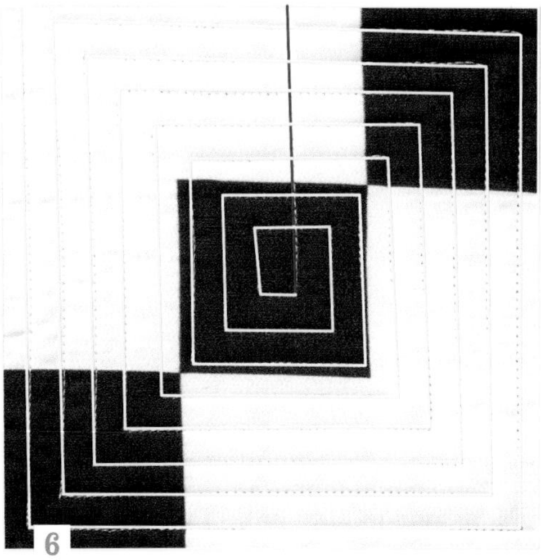

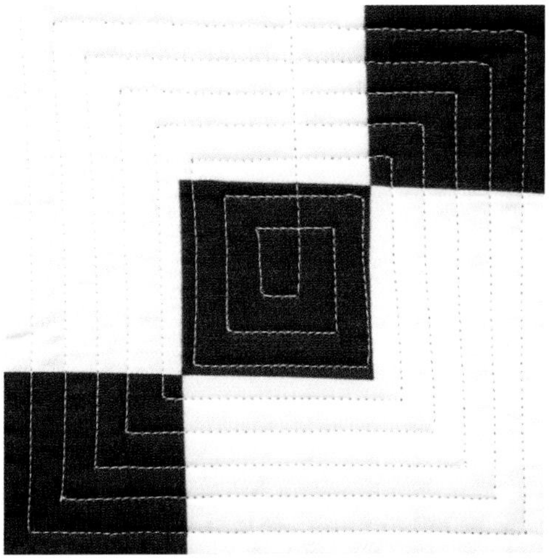

INSIDE TRIANGLE

This fun design is fabulous by itself, but it's also really interesting when it's repeated and rotated. Secondary designs come to life!

STEP 1 • *Use a blue water-soluble pen to mark the top center point.*

STEP 2 • *Beginning in the lower left corner, use a straight machine quilting ruler to stitch a straight line to the top marked point. Turn and stitch to the lower right corner.*

STEP 3 • *From the lower right corner, stitch-in-the-ditch along the bottom of the block to the left side, stopping about ½˝ from the corner. From that point, stitch a straight vertical line from the bottom of the block to the diagonal line.*

STEP 4 • *Travel about ½˝ along the previously stitched diagonal line, then stitch a straight line to the bottom of the block. From that point, travel ½˝ along the ditch, then stitch up to the top diagonal line.*

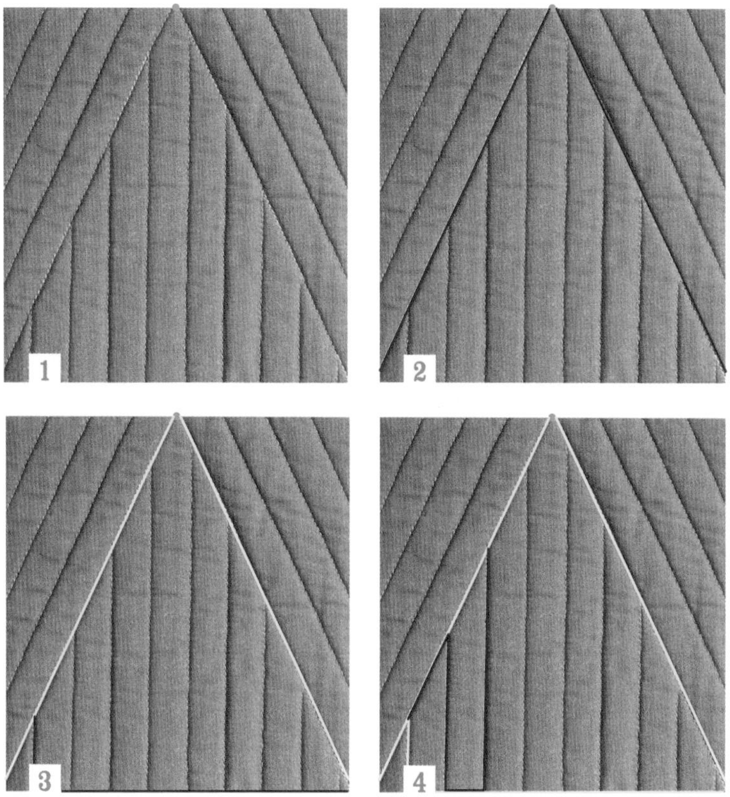

STEP 5 • *Repeat previous steps until the triangle is filled in completely with vertical lines.*

STEP 6 • *From the bottom right corner, travel up the right ditch about ½˝. From that point, turn and stitch a straight line parallel to the top right side of the triangle.*

STEP 7 • *Travel in-the-ditch across the top edge of the block, about ½˝. From that point stitch another parallel diagonal line down to the right side of the block. Repeat this process until you've filled in the top right side of the block completely.*

STEP 8 • *Stitch-in-the-ditch to travel to the top left side of the block. Repeat the process to fill in the top left section with straight lines ½˝ apart.*

Stitch in the ditch all the way around the block.

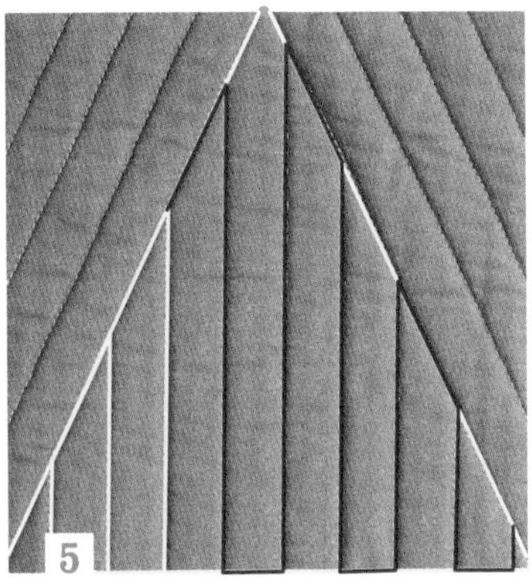

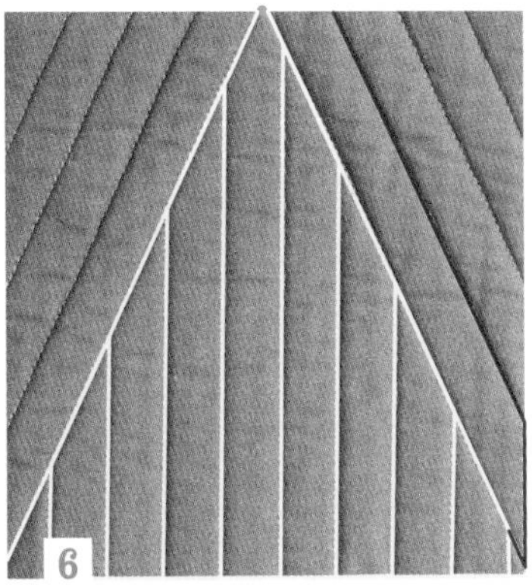

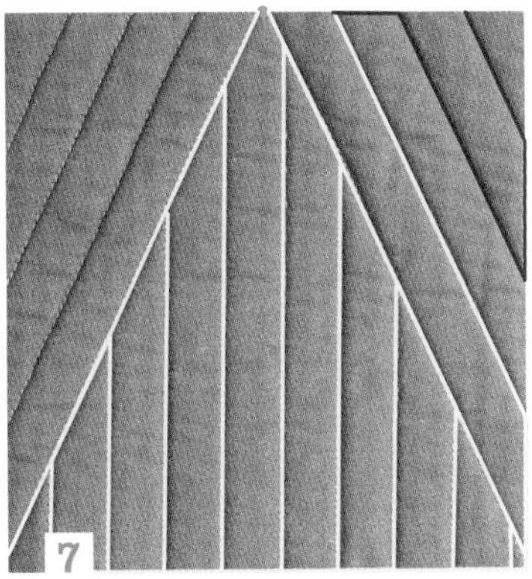

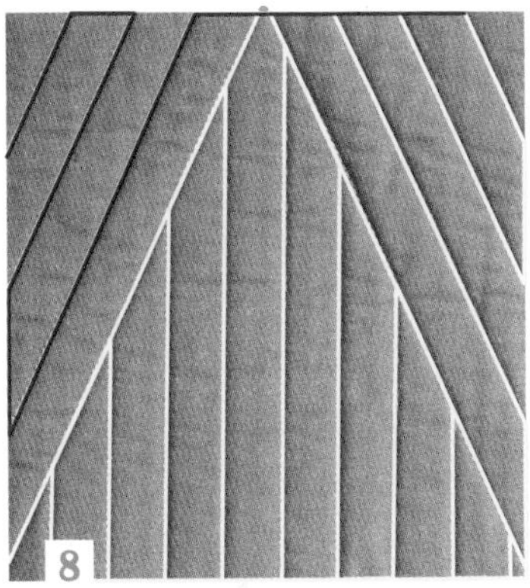

DIMENSIONAL RAYS

The Dimensional Rays design is pretty as a single block. But you could add some heavy fillers in the larger open sections to really create some fabulous texture. This design is also great when four blocks are done together.

STEP 1 • *Start by using a blue water-soluble pen and mark points along the top and right sides of the block. Place the first mark ½˝ from the left side and the second point ½˝ from the previous marking. From that point continue marking every ½˝.*

STEP 2 • *Beginning in the lower left corner, stitch a straight line to the first marked point.*

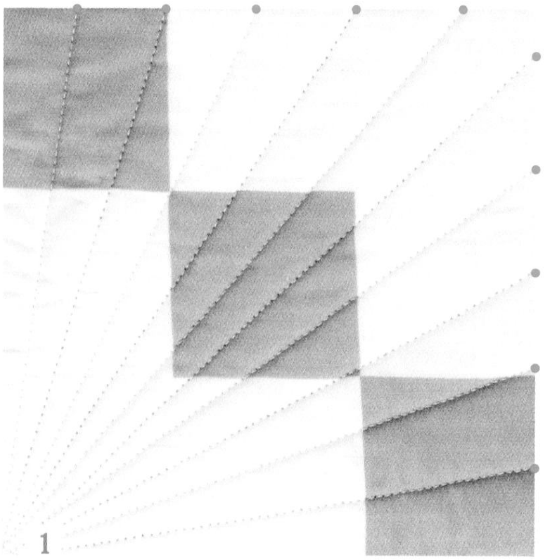

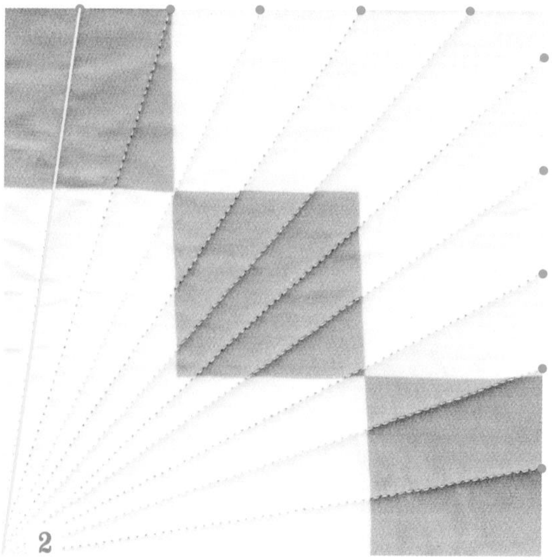

STEP 3 • *Stitch-in-the-ditch along the top of the block to the second marked point. From that point stitch back to the lower left corner.*

STEP 4 • *Repeat the previous steps, stitching point to point, traveling in the ditch along the outside edge to get from point to point. Once you've stitched to all the points stitch-in-the-ditch all the way around the block.*

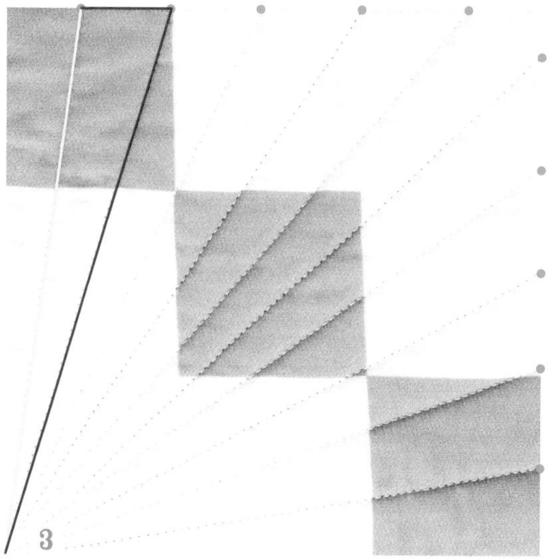

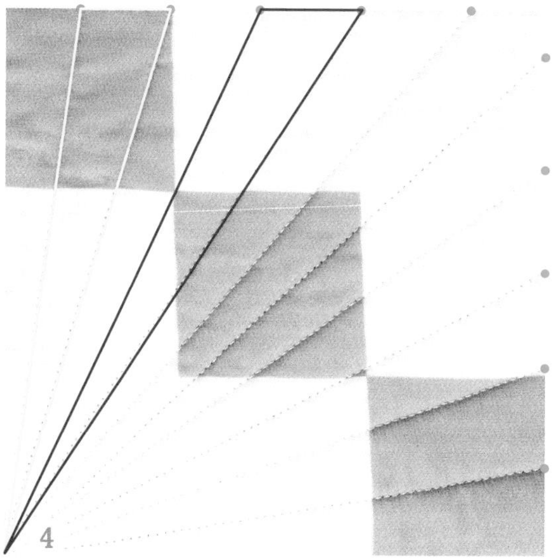

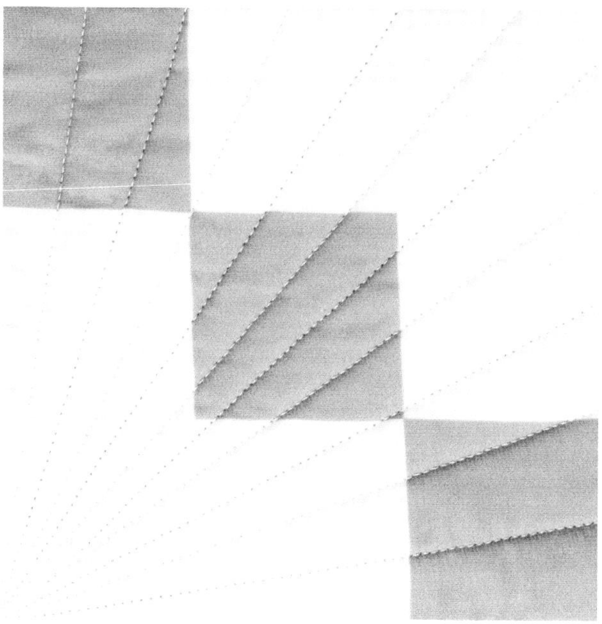

SPINNING PINWHEEL

This design adds a lot of movement to any square or Hourglass-type quilt block. In the block below, the diagram shows just two diagonal lines inside each triangle. If you're quilting this design out on a larger block or just want heavier quilting, simply add more lines or make the spacing between the lines a little bit smaller.

STEP 1 • *Starting in the bottom left corner of the block, stitch a straight line to the upper right corner. From there, stitch-in-the-ditch down the right side of the block to the lower right corner.*

STEP 2 • *From the lower right corner, stitch a diagonal line to the upper left corner.*

STEP 3 • *Use a blue water-soluble pen and mark two points along each of the diagonal lines. The first point should be ½˝ from the outside edge and the second point should be ½˝ from the first point.*

1

2

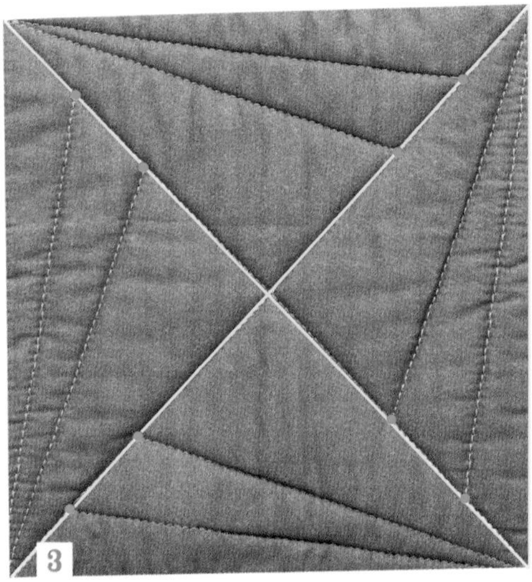
3

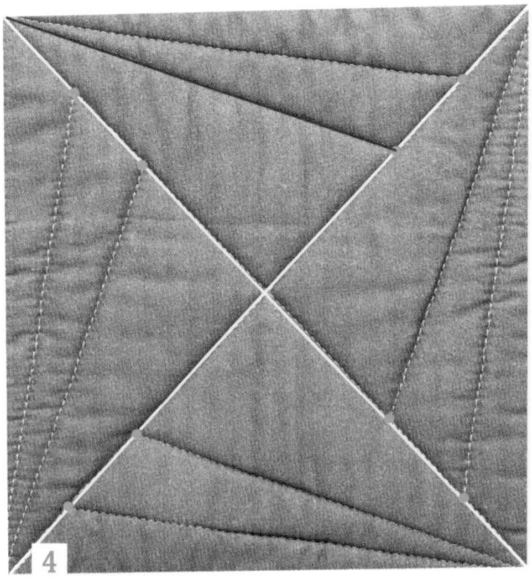

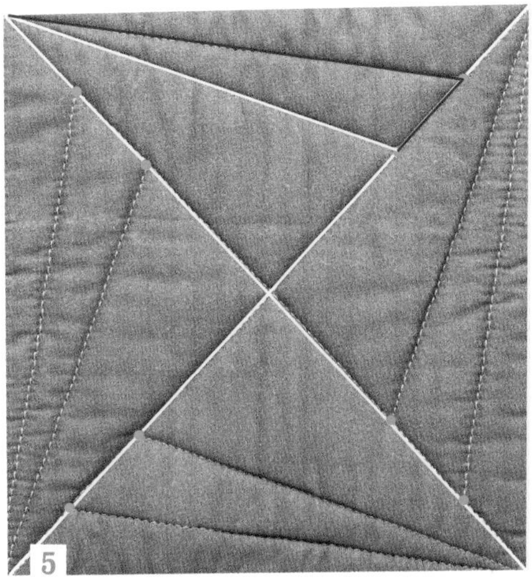

STEP 4 • *From the upper left corner, stitch a straight line to the inner point on the top right top diagonal line.*

STEP 5 • *Travel along the previous stitch line to the outer point on the same diagonal. From that point, stitch a straight line back to the upper left corner.*

STEP 6 • *Stitch-in-the-ditch down to the lower left corner. Then repeat the process in the previous steps to fill in the triangle.*

Continue to travel around the block to fill in the remaining two triangles.

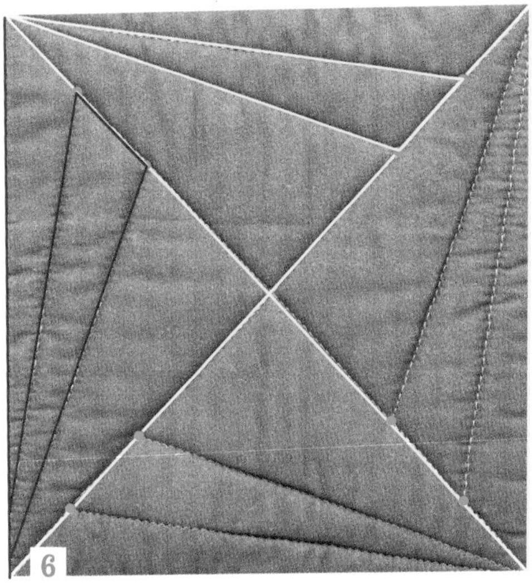

PLAID SQUARE

The plaid square design makes a statement with its simple quilting. But you also can add interest by filling in the center square with pebbles, swirls, or even matchstick-type quilting.

STEP 1 • *Beginning in the upper left corner, stitch-in-the-ditch all the way around the block. When you get back to the upper left corner, travel in-the-ditch about ½˝ down the left side, then use a straight machine quilting ruler to stitch a straight, horizontal line ½˝ below the top edge of the block.*

STEP 2 • *Travel in-the-ditch to the top right corner and ½˝ across the top edge of block. Then stitch a straight, vertical line ½˝ from the right side of the block.*

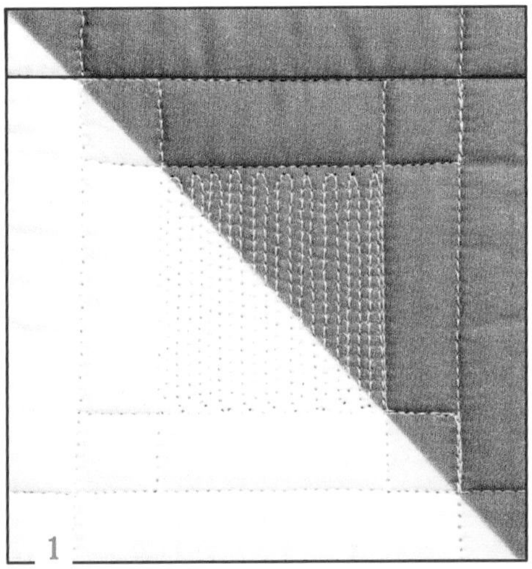

1

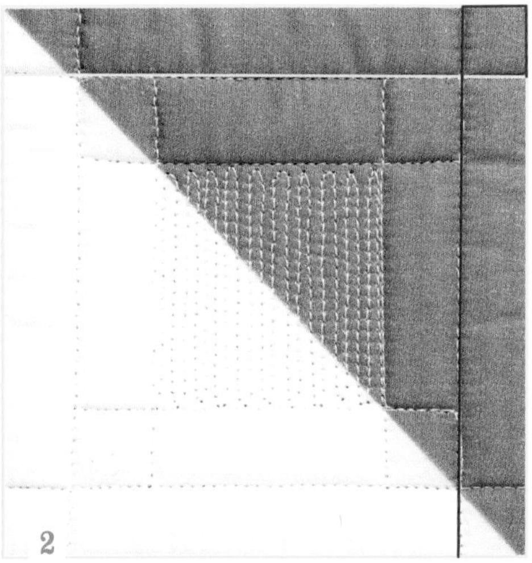

2

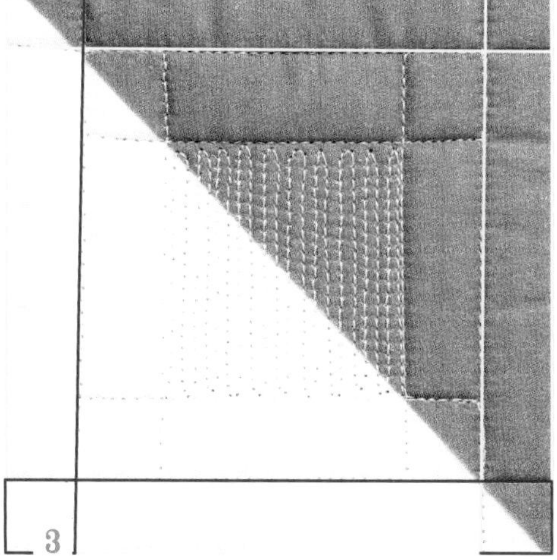

3

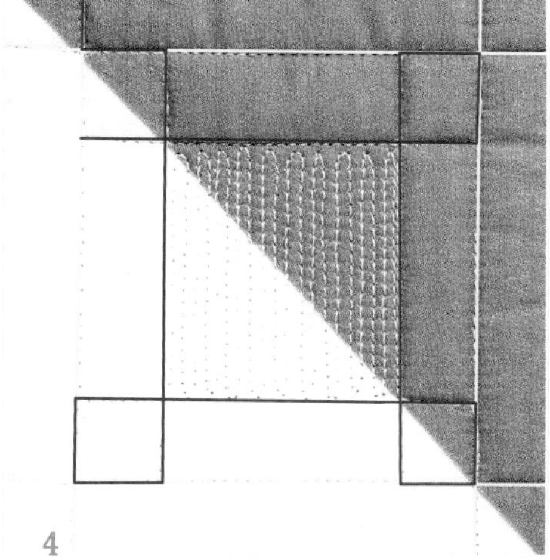

4

STEP 3 • *Travel in-the-ditch to the lower right corner and ½˝ up the right side of the block. Then stitch a straight, horizontal line ½˝ from the bottom of the block.*

Repeat the process to stitch the vertical line at the left edge of the block, ending at the top.

★ Natalia's Tip

On some designs, if you wanted to be a bit more modern you could leave the block quilted with just two sides.

STEP 4 • *From the top, travel along the previous stitch line, moving about 1˝ toward the bottom of the block. From that point, stitch out the same design that as Steps 1–3, just on a smaller scale at the center of the block.*

STEP 5 • *Move to the center of the block and stitch small straight lines to create extra texture.*

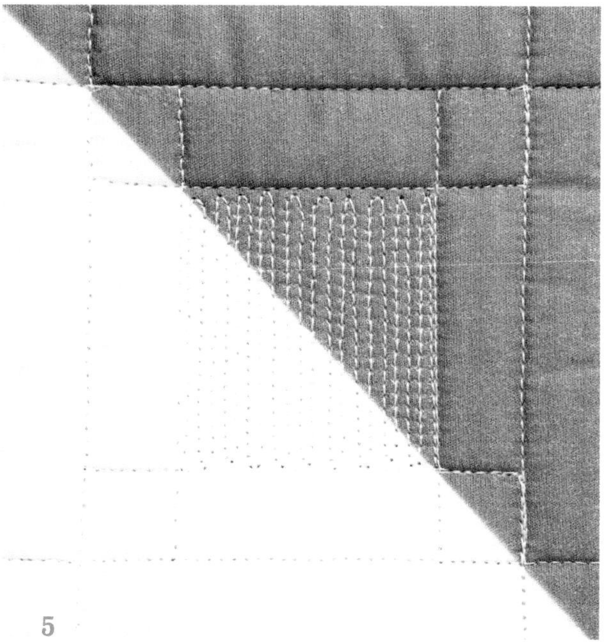

5

DISAPPEARING SQUARE

The Disappearing Square is a great design by itself. But it's also fabulous when four blocks are put together and quilted with the 90° angles at the center. The secondary designs that come to life can really make a simple design fantastic.

STEP 1 • *Begin by stitching a diagonal line through the center of the block, from the bottom left corner to the upper right corner.*

STEP 2 • *From the upper right corner stitch along the top ditch moving toward the left about ½″. From that point using the markings on a straight machine quilting ruler, stitch a second diagonal line, parallel to the first one, from the upper right to the lower left.*

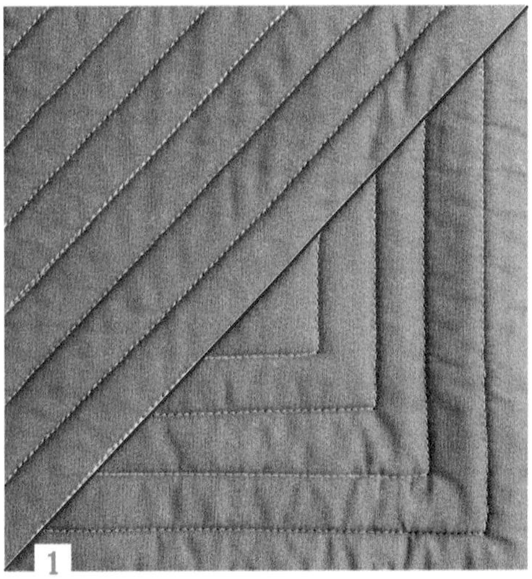

1

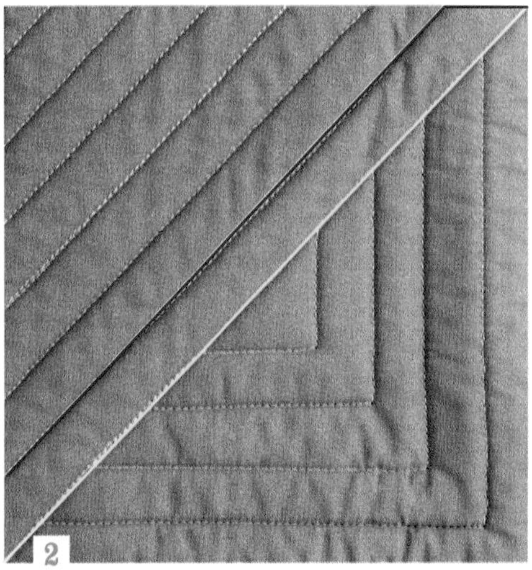

2

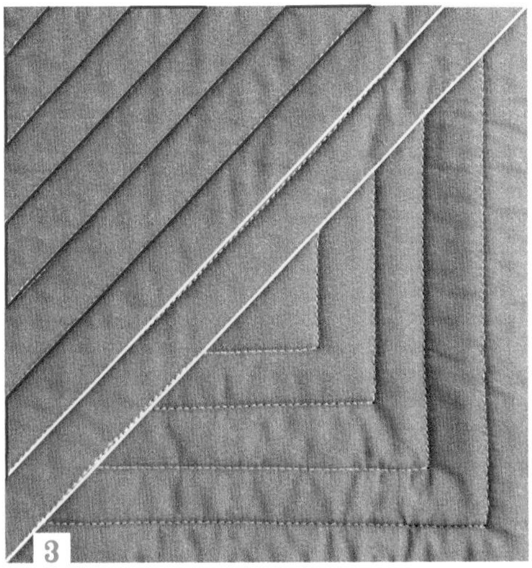

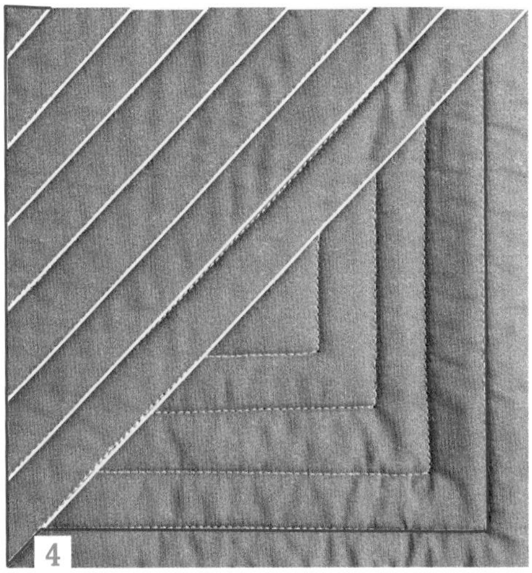

STEP 3 • *From the lower left, travel ½˝ up the ditch and repeat the diagonal line. Continue this process until you've filled in the top half of the block completely with diagonal lines.*

STEP 4 • *Stitch-in-the-ditch from the upper left corner down to the bottom left corner. From that point, travel ½˝ up the diagonal center line. Turn and stitch a straight line parallel to the bottom edge of the block. When you get ½˝ from the right side of the block, turn and stitch a straight vertical line up to the top diagonal line.*

STEP 5 • *Travel ½˝ down the center diagonal line. From that point, turn and stitch a straight vertical line. When you get ½˝ from the previous stitch line, turn and stitch a second horizontal line, stitching all the way to the diagonal line. Repeat, until you've filled in the bottom half of the block completely.*

STEP 6 • *Stitch-in-the-ditch around the entire block.*

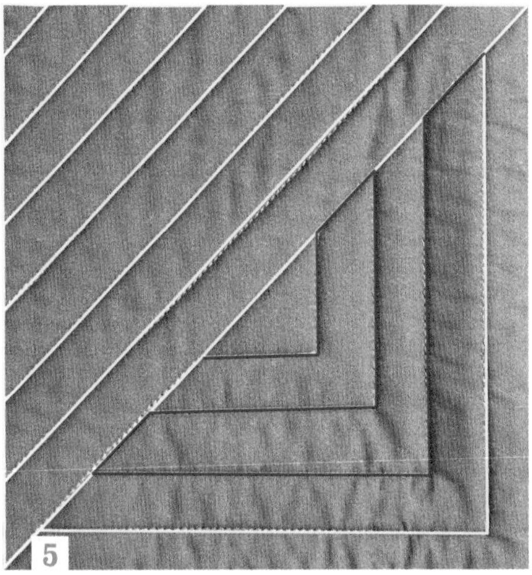

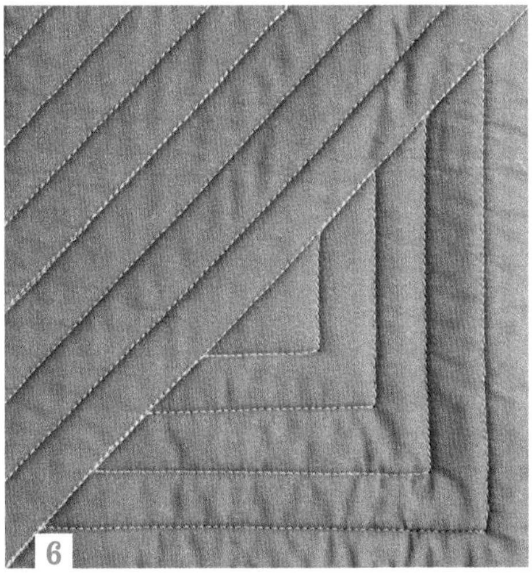

ARGYLE

The Argyle design is a great way to add a bit of dimension to any quilt block. This block could easily have secondary fillers in every other square to create even more texture.

STEP 1 • *Use a blue water-soluble pen to mark a center point on all four sides of the block.*

★ Natalia's Tip

If the block is a pieced block, you could use the pieced seams as your marking instead of marking.

STEP 2 • *Beginning in the upper left corner, stitch a diagonal line from the upper left to the lower right. From that point, stitch-in-the-ditch along the right side of the block to the upper right corner.*

STEP 3 • *Stitch a diagonal line to the lower left corner.*

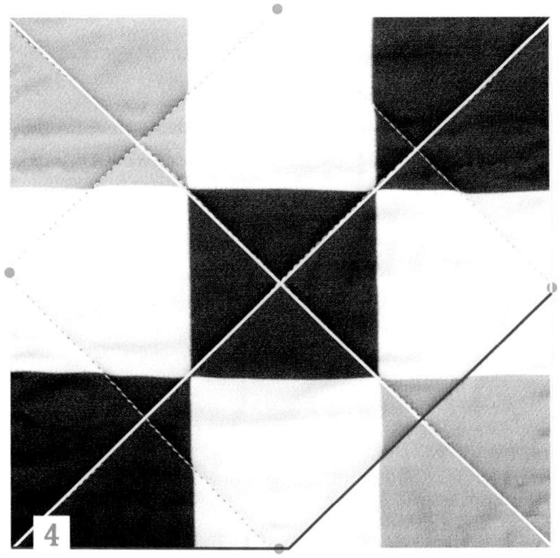

STEP 4 • *Stitch-in-the-ditch along the bottom of the block to the center marked point. From that point, stitch a diagonal line to the marked point on the right side of the block.*

STEP 5 • *From the right side, stitch a straight line to the marked point at the top of the block, then to the center point on the left side of the block and then back the bottom center point.*

STEP 6 • *Stitch-in-the-ditch all the way around the edge of the block.*

MEET IN THE MIDDLE

This fun design creates a lot of great texture. There is a lot of quilting involved, so take your time but have fun with it.

STEP 1 • *Use a blue water-soluble pen to mark 2 intersecting lines through the center of the block.*

★ *Natalia's Tip*

If you prefer not to draw an X through the center of the block, you can stitch the X instead.

STEP 2 • *Beginning in the upper left corner, stitch small back and forth horizontal straight lines from the left side of the block to the marked line, filling in the triangle area completely.*

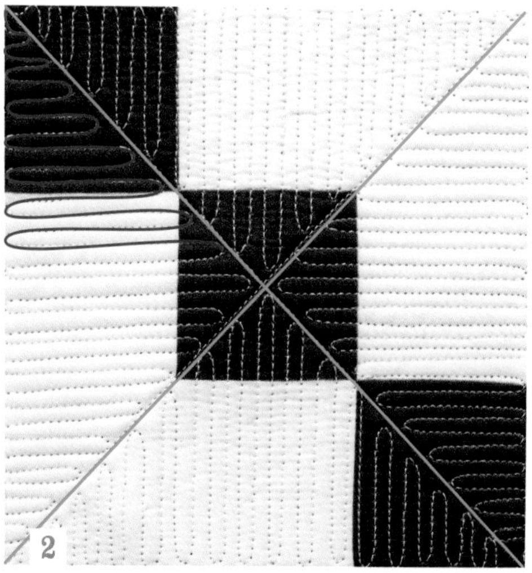

★ *Natalia's Tips*

- I like to use a machine quilting ruler while I stitch out these straight lines. This can be done without, but the ruler helps me keep them straight.
- For great results keep the little lines close. I prefer to keep mine no more than ⅛″ apart.

STEP 3 • *From the bottom corner, stitch vertical straight lines to fill in the bottom triangle.*

Repeat this process, stitching vertical lines in the top and bottom triangles and horizontal lines in the 2 side triangles.

STEP 4 • *Stitch-in-the-ditch all the way around the edge of the block. Spritz away the blue marked lines.*

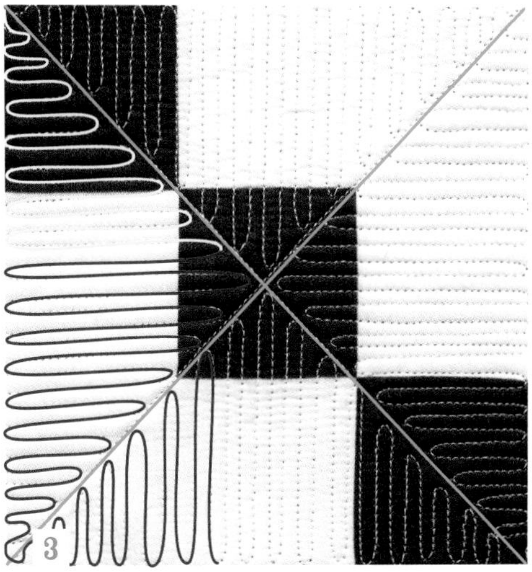

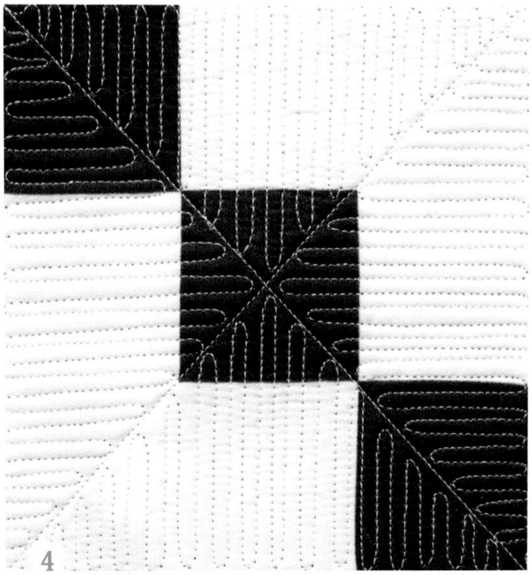

Meet in the Middle Variation

On this design, I've stitched the heavy straight lines in just two of the triangles. I like doing this to create more contrast with the dimension.

BLOCKS INSIDE

This design adds a lot of interest and fun detail to any quilt. I'd recommend using this design on a lightly pieced or solid quilt block.

STEP 1 • *Use a blue water-soluble pen to mark a horizontal and a vertical line through the center of the block.*

STEP 2 • *Beginning on the left side, stitch a horizontal straight line ¼″ above the blue marked line. When you get to the right side of the block, stitch ½″ in-the-ditch down the right side, then stitch a second horizontal line from right to left.*

STEP 3 • *Travel in-the-ditch up the left side, around the corner, and ¼″ past the blue marked line. Stitch a straight vertical line ¼″ from the blue line, stopping when you reach the horizontal stitched line. Stitch along the previous stitch line ½″ to the left, ¼″ past the blue line. Stitch a straight line back to the top of the block.*

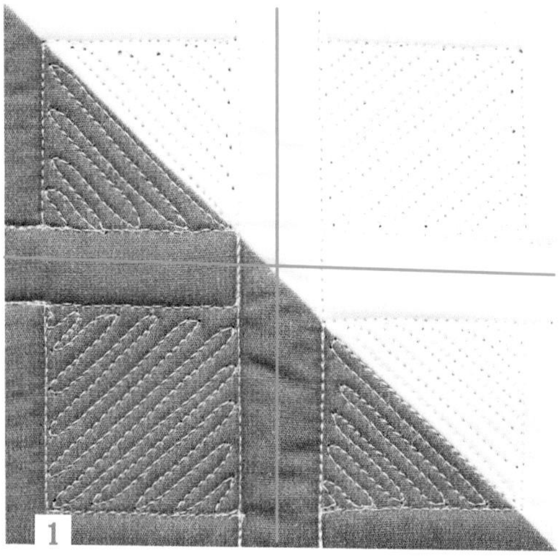

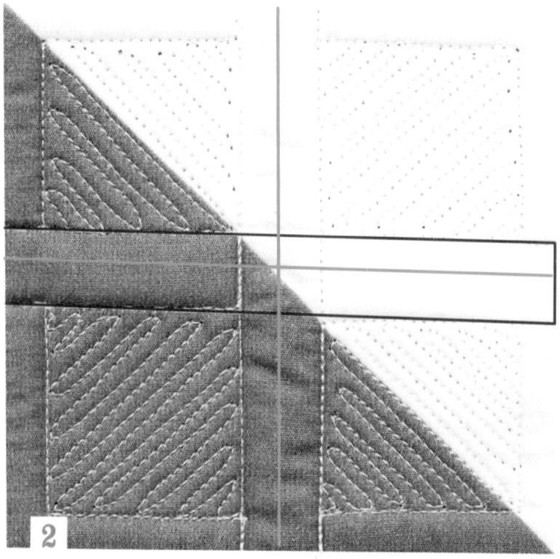

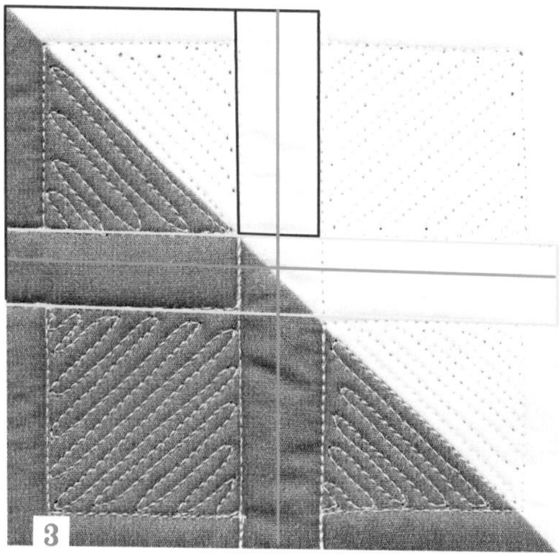

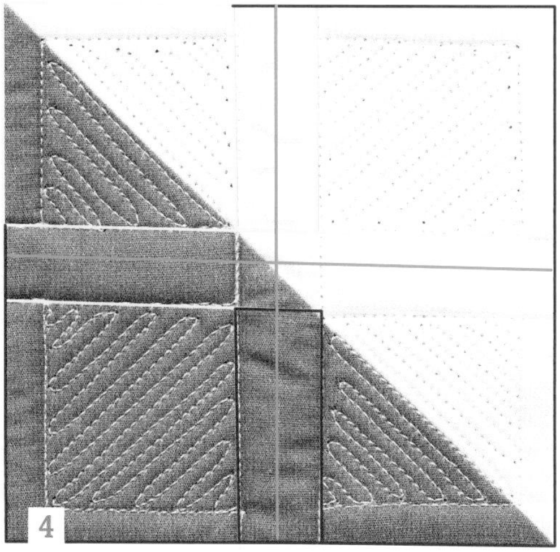

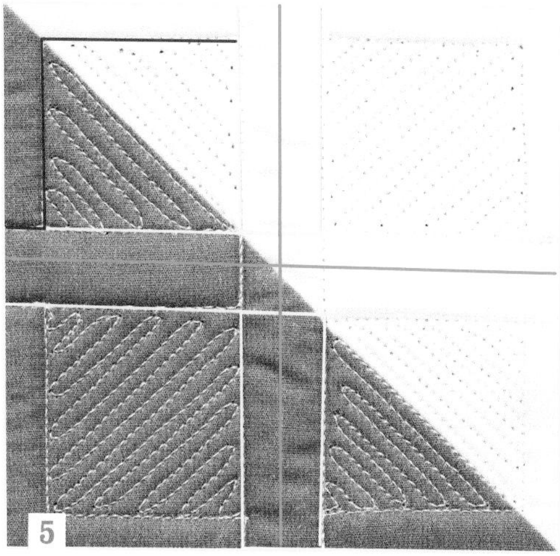

STEP 4 • *Stitch-in-the-ditch along the top edge of the block, down the right side, and across the bottom, stopping ¼˝ past the blue marked line. Stitch a straight vertical line, ¼˝ to the left of the blue line, stopping when you reach the horizontal stitched line. Stitch along the previous stitch line to the right, ¼˝ past the blue line. Stitch a straight line back the bottom of the block.*

From that point stitch-in-the ditch along the bottom of the block and then back up the left side to the original starting point.

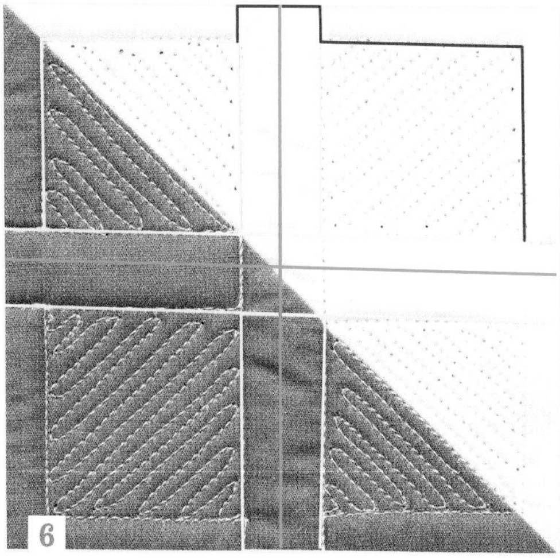

STEP 5 • *Travel along the first stitched line, moving in ¼˝. From that point, stitch a straight vertical line, stopping ¼˝ from the top of the block, then stitch a horizontal line stopping at the stitch line.*

★ *Natalia's Tip*

If you like heavier quilting with a lot of texture, from this point fill in the open square with heavy matchstick quilting. In the sample I quilted the matchstick quilting on the diagonal to create even more interest.

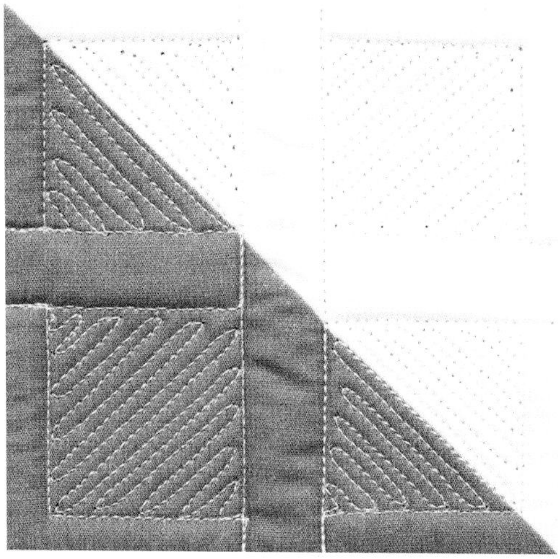

STEP 6 • *Use the process in Step 5 to stitch the remaining 3 outside squares within the frame.*

DOUBLE DIAMOND

The Double Diamond design almost creates a star.
This design is great on most quilt types.

STEP 1 • *Use a blue water-soluble pen to mark an X through the center of the block. Here you need to mark only 1 diagonal of the X. The block's seam creates the other diagonal for you. Then mark 4 points along the X line, each ½″ from the edge of the block.*

STEP 2 • *Beginning in the upper left corner, stitch a straight line to the upper right marked point, and then down to the lower right corner.*

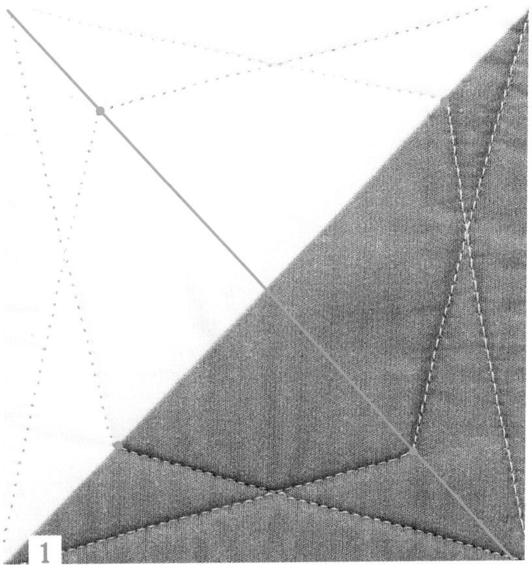

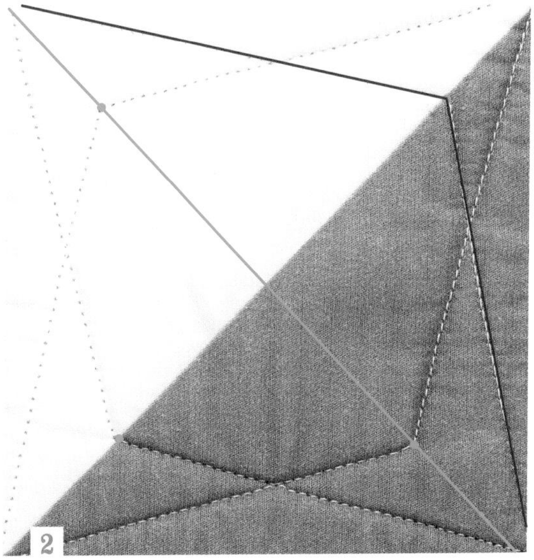

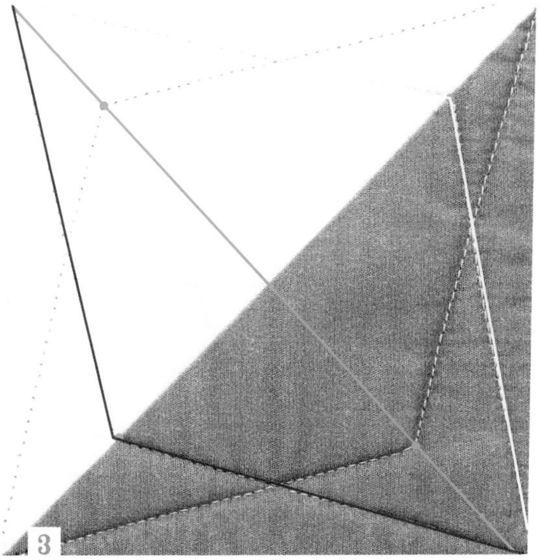

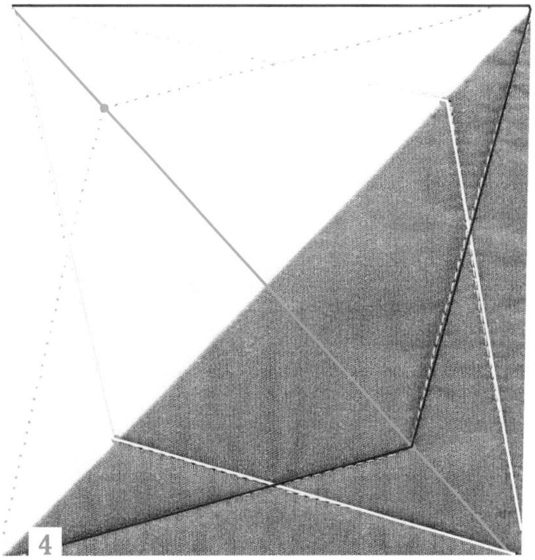

STEP 3 · *Stitch a straight line to the lower left marked point, and then up to the upper left corner.*

STEP 4 · *Travel in-the-ditch along the top of the block to the upper right corner. From the upper right corner, stitch a straight line to the lower right point, then to the lower left corner. From the lower left corner, stitch to the upper left marked point and then back to the upper right corner.*

Stitch-in-the ditch around the remaining sides of the block.

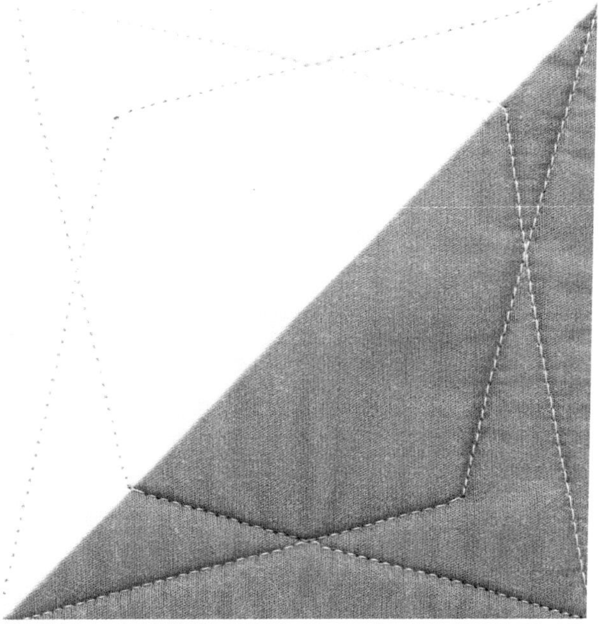

SQUARES IN SQUARES

Squares in Squares is really cute quilted just like the design shown, but you could always go back and add in secondary designs to create some fun details.

STEP 1 • *Use a blue water-soluble pen to mark the center point on all 4 sides of the block.*

STEP 2 • *Beginning at the top center, stitch-in-the-ditch all the way around the block. When you get back to the top center, stitch to the marked point on the right side of the block, then to the bottom center point, then to the left marked point, and then back to the top center point.*

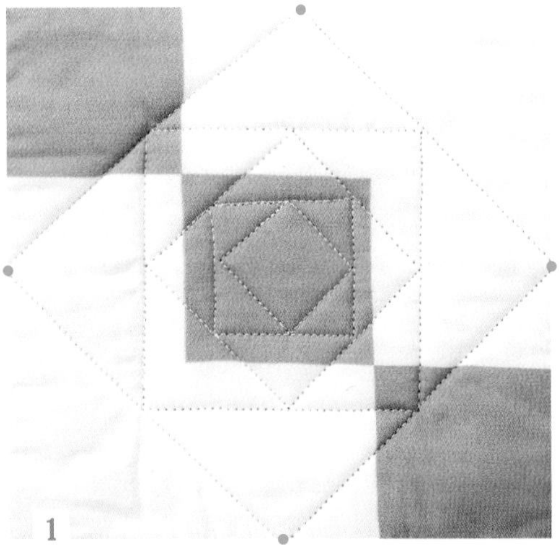

1

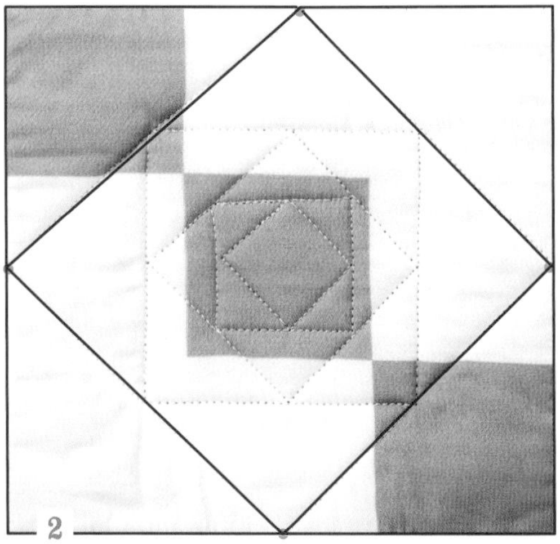

2

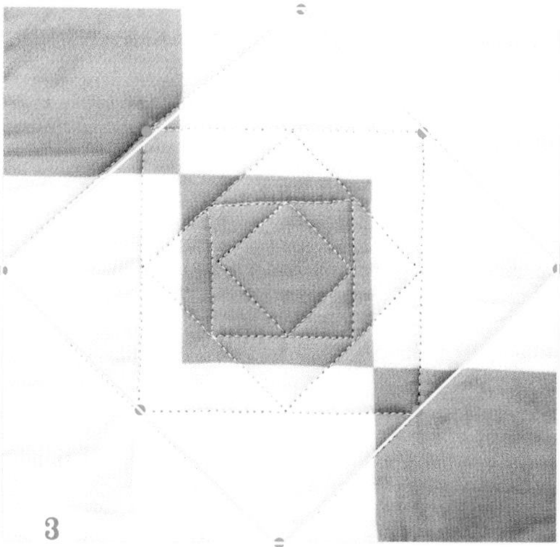

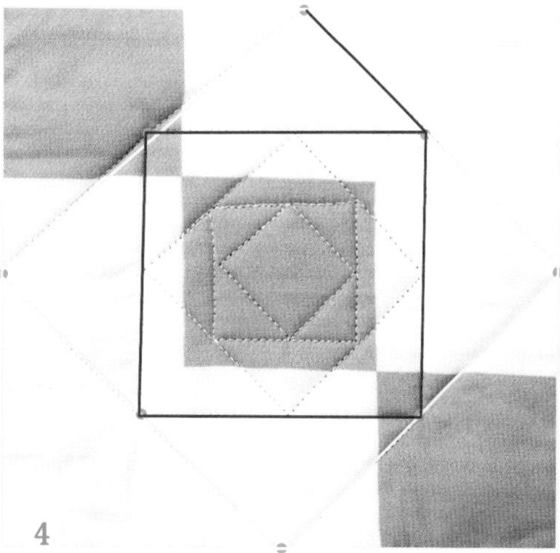

STEP 3 • *Use a blue water-soluble pen to mark the center points along all 4 sides of the square that you stitched in the previous step.*

STEP 4 • *From the top center point, stitch along the previous stitch line to the point between the left and top sides. From that point, stitch a straight line to the upper right point, then the lower right point, then to the lower left point, and then back to the upper left point.*

★ *Natalia's Tip*

If you want heavier quilting repeat the previous steps to continue stitching squares in squares.

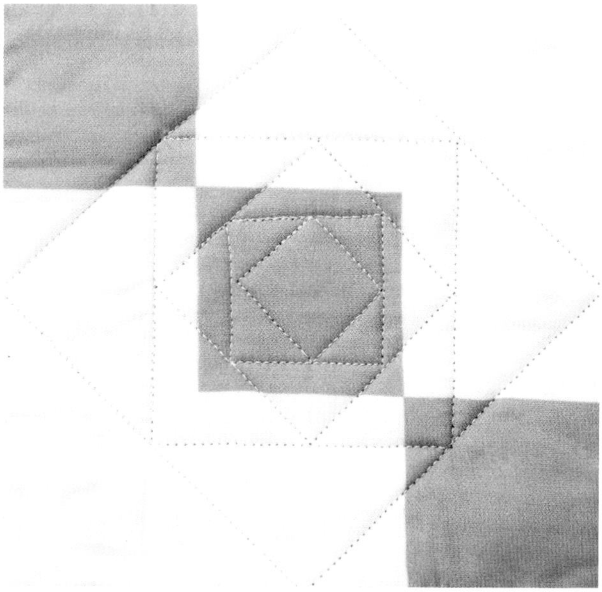

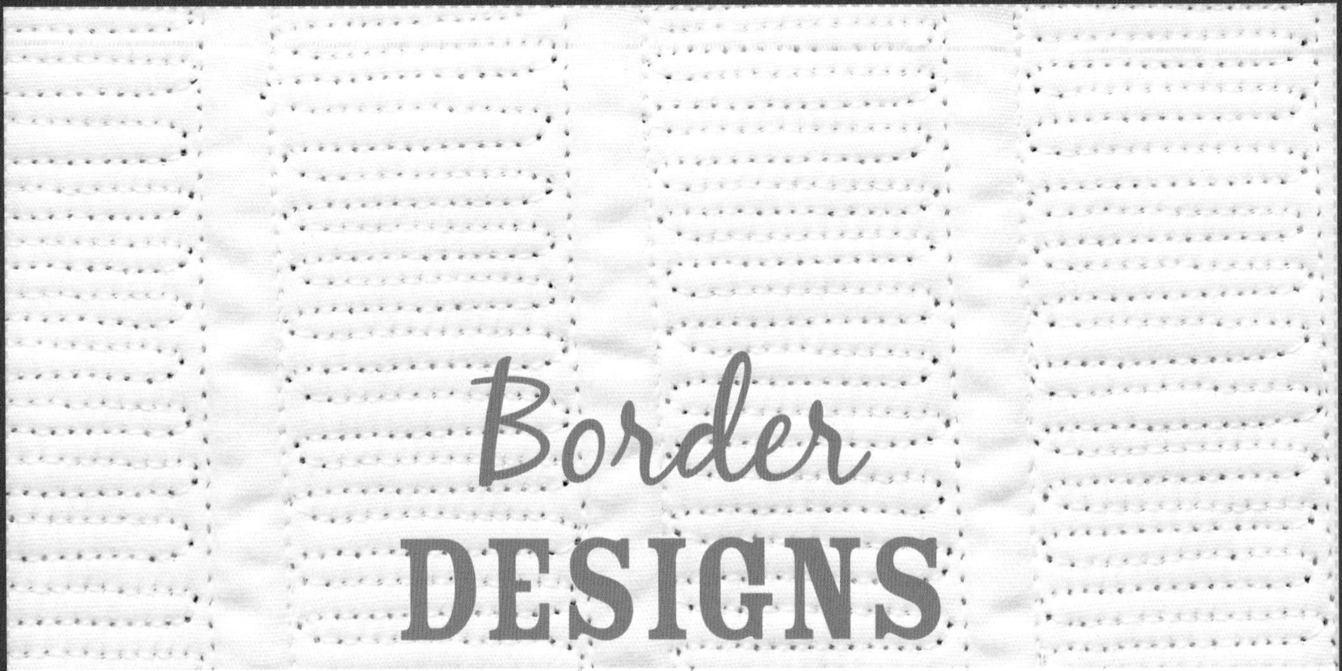

Border DESIGNS

Borders can be beautiful with straight lines too! Sometimes simple straight lines like Piano Keys are the perfect fit. Other times, you may want something with a bit more detail like the Weave design. All the designs in this chapter are stitched with straight lines. A little bit of ruler work and/or marking and you'll have beautiful, crisp, clean border designs.

PIANO KEYS

The Piano Keys designs is simple but can be dressed up with fillers to create great texture. The repetitive design also gives the eye a place to rest.

★ *Natalia's Tip*

You could mark the piano keys design before you begin stitching. I prefer to use the markings on my machine quilting ruler and not actually do any marking on the quilt for this design.

STEP 1 • *Begin by stitching a straight line from the edge of the quilt to the border seam. I begin stitching on the outside and work to the inside.*

STEP 2 • *At the border seam, stitch 1˝ over in-the-ditch. Turn and stitch a second straight line, parallel to the first.*

STEP 3 • *When you reach the edge of the border, stitch 1˝ over in-the-ditch, then stitch a third parallel line. Repeat this process until you've filled in the border with piano keys.*

1

2

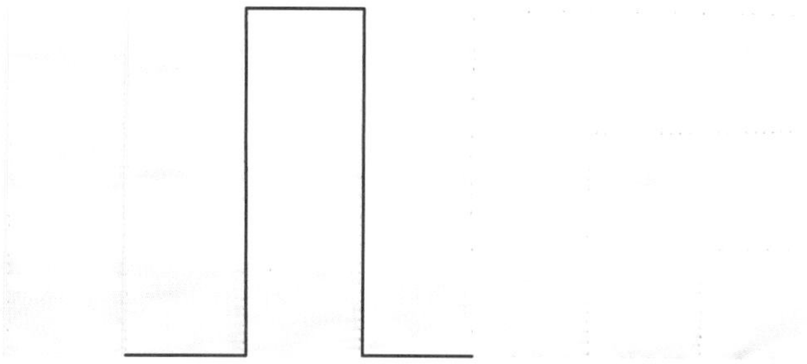

3

STEP 4 • *When you get to the corner, use a blue water-soluble pen to mark a 45° angle from the inside point to the outer corner.*

Marking border corners is the same whether you stitch the simple Piano Keys in the original instructions, or the fancier version shown in the Piano Keys Variation (next page).

4

STEP 5 • *Stitch a straight vertical line from the outside to the inside, then turn and stitch a straight line to the other side of the quilt corner.*

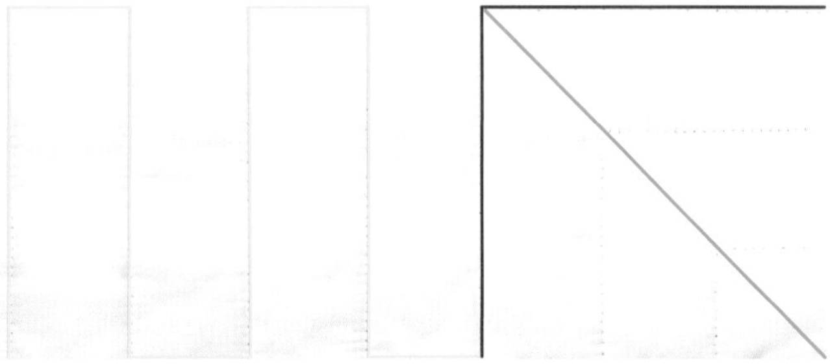

5

STEP 6 • *Stitch-in-the-ditch 1˝ down. From that point, stitch a parallel line stopping at the diagonal marked line. Turn and stitch a straight line down to the outside border, keeping that line 1˝ from the previous stitch line.*

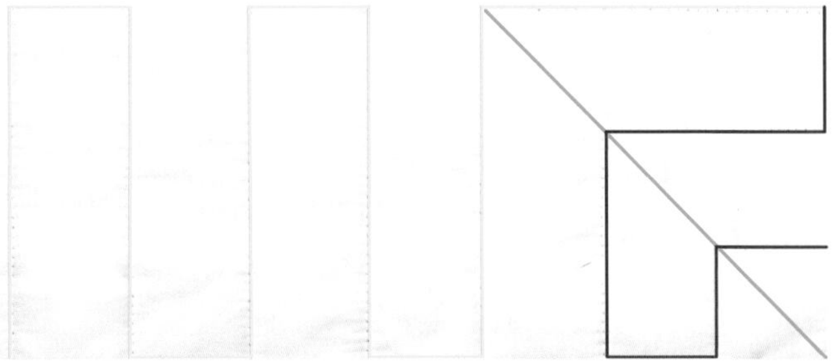

6

STEP 7 · *Repeat the previous steps until you've filled in the border corner completely. Spritz away the blue marked lines. Stitch-in-the-ditch all the way around the border.*

7

Piano Keys Variation

To add more interest to your Piano Key border, add fills to every other open space. On the variation shown here, I used a heavy horizontal straight-line fill. Doing this creates a lot of dimension and gives more texture to the border design.

SIMPLE LINES

The Simple Lines design can give a bit of an elegant look to your border or sashing. To add texture, fill in the larger open areas with a heavy filler like pebbles or matchstick quilting.

★ *Natalia's Tip*

You could mark the design on the border before you start stitching. I prefer to use the markings on my machine quilting ruler and not actually do any marking on the quilt for this design.

STEP 1 • *Begin stitching a straight line. I begin stitching on the outer edge and work to the inside.*

STEP 2 • *From the inside point, stitch-in-the-ditch, traveling over ¼″. Turn and stitch a second straight line, parallel to the first.*

STEP 3 • *At the outer edge, stitch 1″ in-the-ditch, then turn and stitch a third parallel line. Repeat this process until you've filled in the border with simple lines.*

1

2

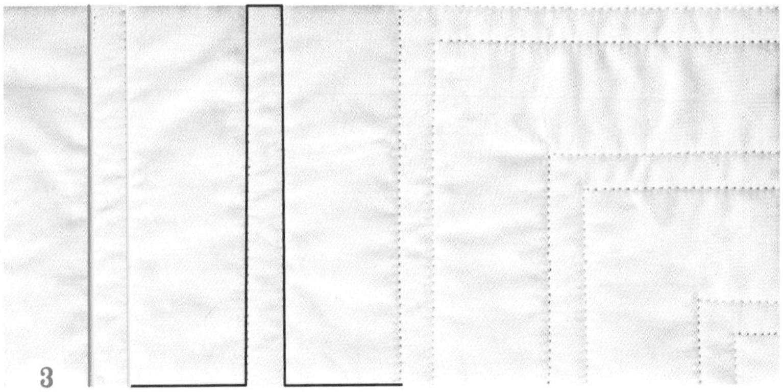

3

STEP 4 • *At the corner use a blue water-soluble pen to mark a 45° angle, from the inside point to the outside. See the instructions for stitching a border corner in Piano Keys, Steps 4–6 (page 96).*

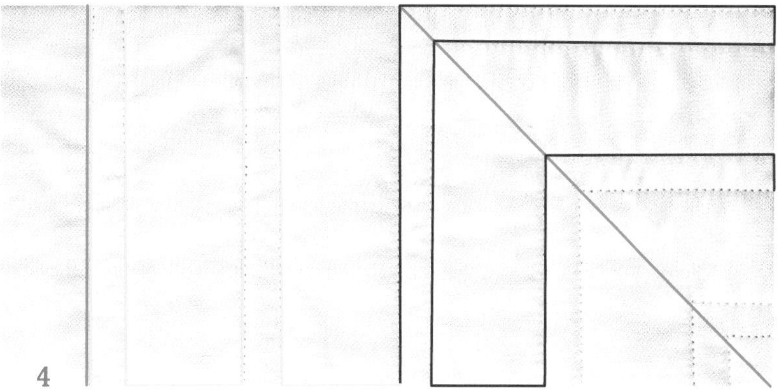

Simple Lines Variation

Fill in the larger open areas with back-and-forth stitching to add texture.

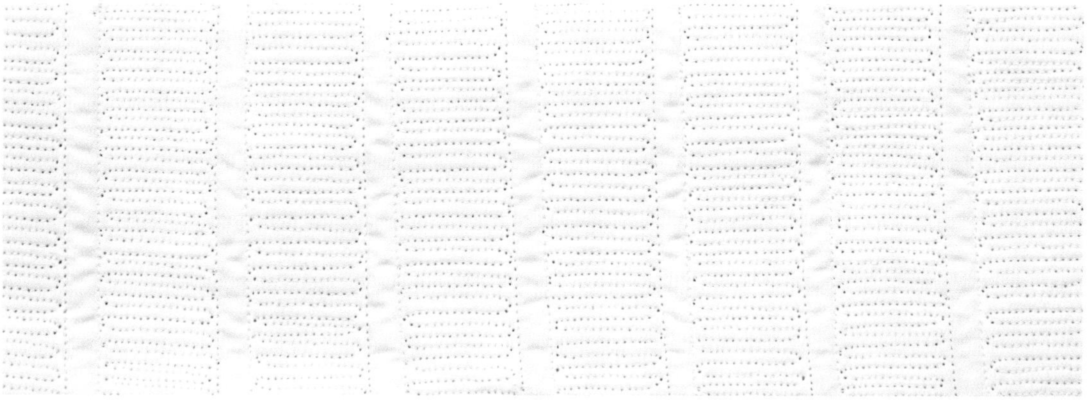

CHEVRON

The Chevron is a great way to add a little bit of geometric movement to a border or sashing. When marking and stitching this design in an outer border, make sure to take into consideration that you'll lose about ¼˝ to the binding.

STEP 1 • *Use a blue water-soluble pen to mark a straight line through the center of the border.*

★ Natalia's Tip

To find the center of an outer border, I like to mark a line ¼˝ from the edge of the border, all the way around the quilt. From there, I'll measure the border width to find the center of the border.

STEP 2 • *Mark straight lines 1˝ apart all along the border.*

STEP 3 • *Starting at the left end of a border, stitch a straight line from the inside point to the center marked point, then to the outer marked point at the edge of the quilt or sashing.*

1

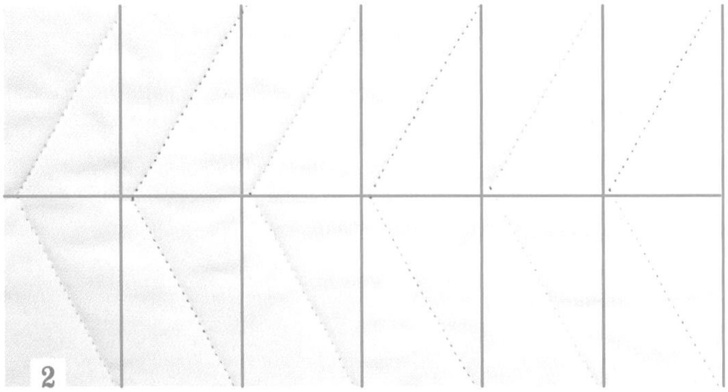

2

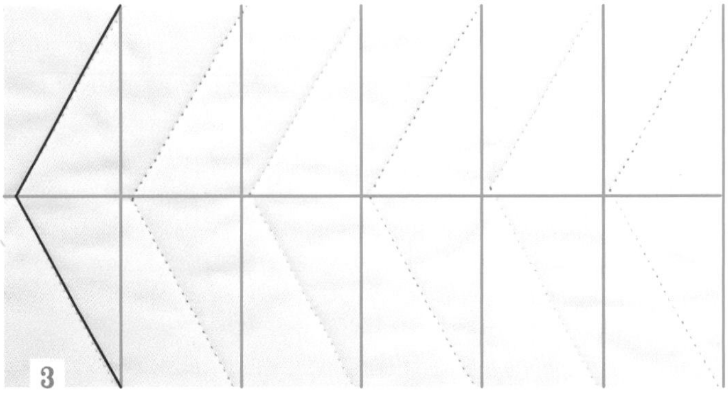

3

STEP 4 • *Stitch-in-the-ditch along the bottom edge to the next marked point. From that point, stitch a diagonal line to the center marked point and then back to the top side of the border.*

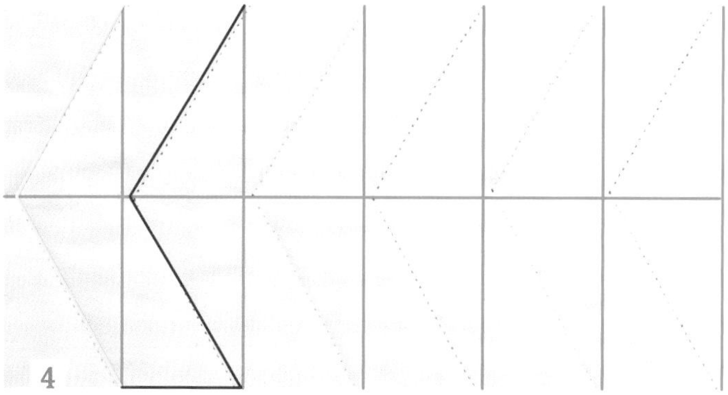

STEP 5 • *Repeat the previous steps until you've stitched the entire border design. Stitch-in-the-ditch all the way around the border. Spritz away the blue markings.*

Chevron Variation

In this Chevron variation, I've filled in every other space with heavy straight-line quilting.

WEAVE

The Weave design gives any border a woven look. This design can appear to be much more complicated than it actually is.

STEP 1 • *Measure the total finished length and width of the border. In general, if the border is 6˝ wide, plan to make your triangles 6˝ to completely fill the space. The size may vary slightly depending on the quilt.*

STEP 2 • *Mark the inner edge of the border in increments of 6˝, or whatever triangle width you have chosen.*

STEP 3 • *Mark the outside edge of the border with increments every 6˝, but start the first marking at 3˝.*

STEP 4 • *From the lower left point, stitch point-to-point straight lines creating a zigzag look all the way through the border.*

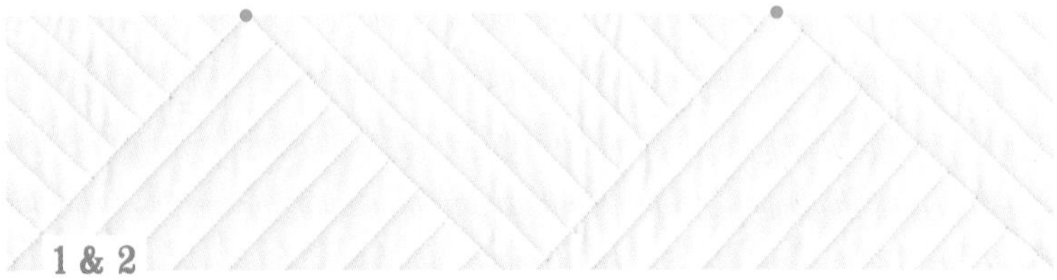

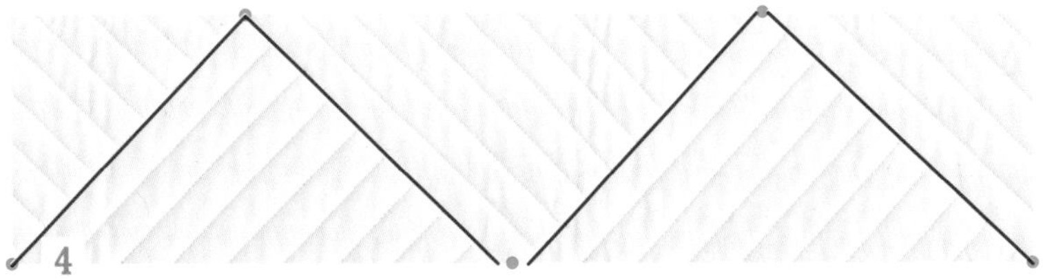

STEP 5 • *Start filling in the triangles with straight lines. Start stitching in the lower left and stitch a straight line on the first diagonal line. When you reach the opposite stitched line, travel along the line about ½″, then stitch another parallel line back to the outer edge of the border.*

Repeat this process until you've filled in the triangle completely.

STEP 6 • *Move to the next triangle and repeat the same process that you stitched in the first triangle, filling in the triangle completely with straight lines.*

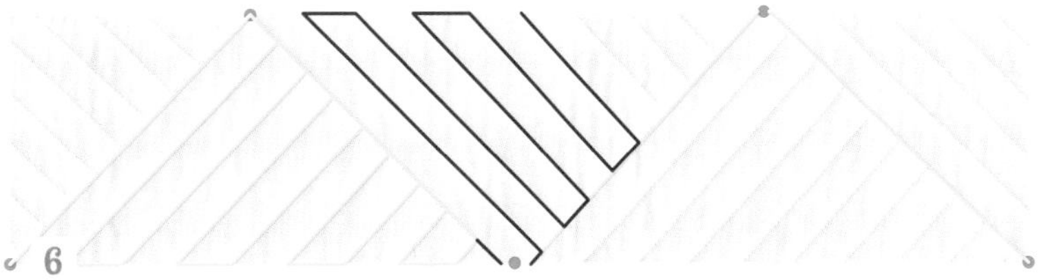

Repeat this process until you've filled in all the triangles completely.

RAILROAD

In the Railroad design, the simple spacing that borders the straight lines gives the eye a place to rest while creating even more interest.

STEP 1 • *Begin by stitching a straight line parallel to the long edge of the border, ¼˝ away from each edge.*

1

★ Natalia's Tip

If you're quilting this design on an outside border, make sure that you leave enough space for the binding. You don't want to lose the outside of this design in the binding. (See Chevron, Natalia's Tip, page 100.)

STEP 2 • *Starting at the left end of the border, stitch a straight line perpendicular to the straight lines stitched in Step 1.*

STEP 3 • *Travel along the previous stitch line ½˝ to the right. From that point turn and stitch another straight line parallel to the line in Step 2.*

2

3

STEP 4 • *Repeat Steps 2 and 3 until you have filled in the border. To add more interest, you could adjust the spacing between lines.*

4

Railroad Variation

This variation is stitched with the same techniques but is quilted on point to create more interest.

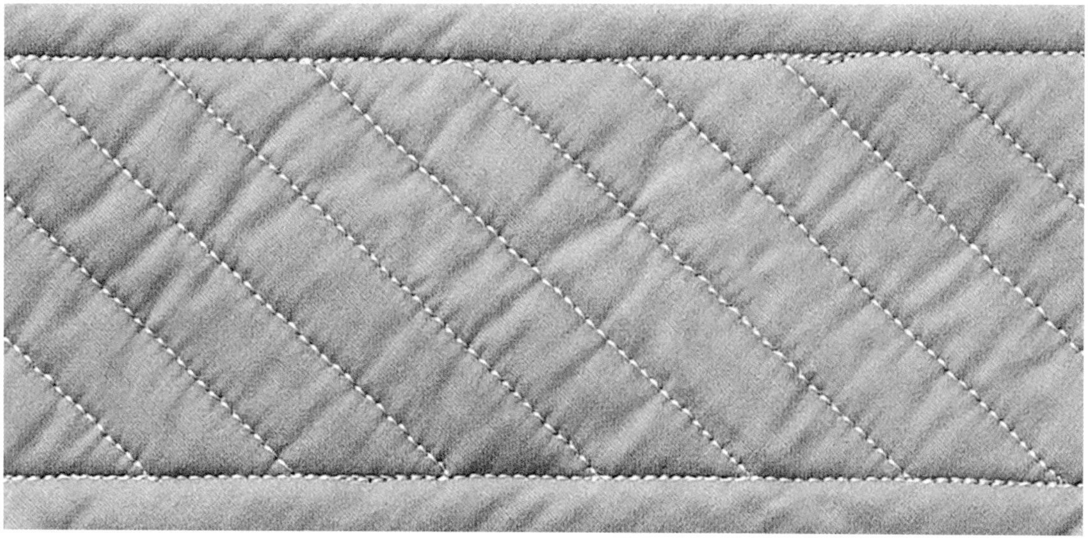

MERGE

The Merge design is a great way to keep a border simple yet have a little bit of flair down the center. This design would look really cute with figure eights or pebbles quilted through the center. The measurements here are for a border that is at least 3″ wide. For a smaller or larger border, you will need to adjust your measurements accordingly.

STEP 1 • *Stitch a straight line 1″ from each side of the border.*

STEP 2 • *Stitch a straight line ½″ closer to the center than the previous stitch line.*

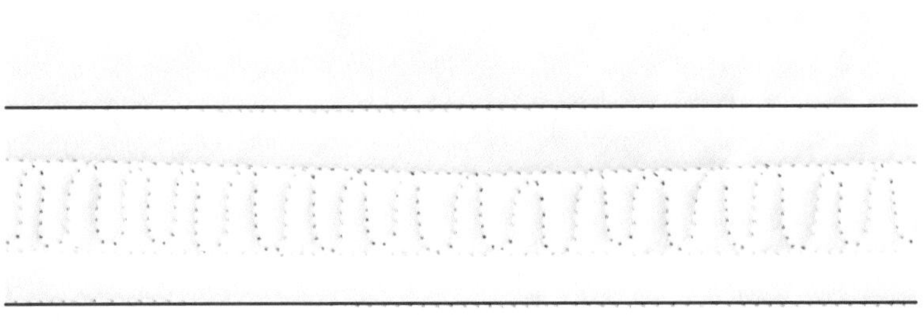

1

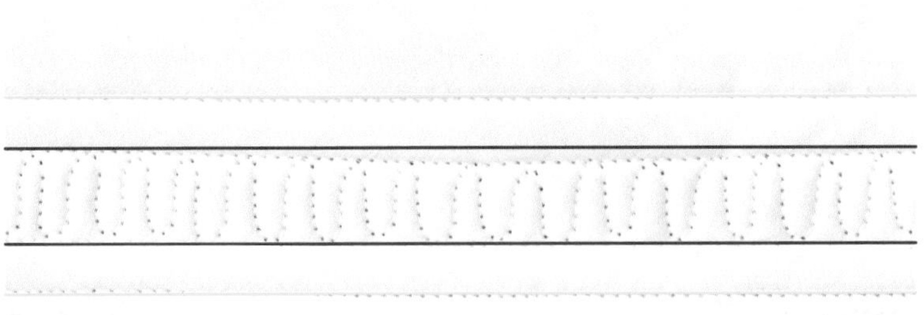

2

STEP 3 • *Stitch a small curved straight-line design through the remaining center space in the border.*

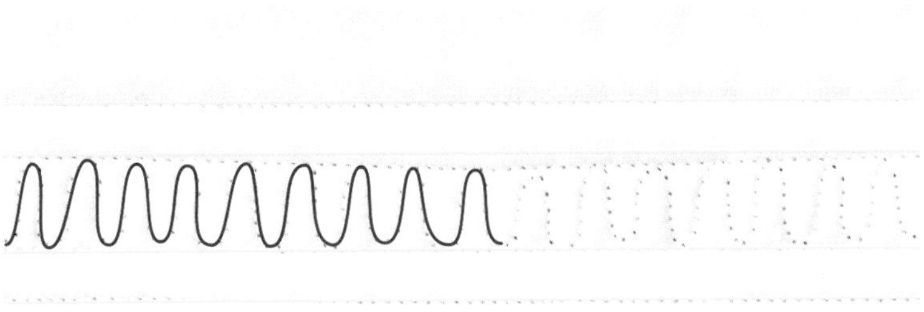

3

Merge Variation

In the Merge variation, the spacing has simply been adjusted. The first lines are ½˝ from the outer edges, the second lines are 1˝ from the previous lines, and the next lines are ½˝ from the previous stitch line. To finish, stitch a small curved straight-line design through each of the 1˝ spaces.

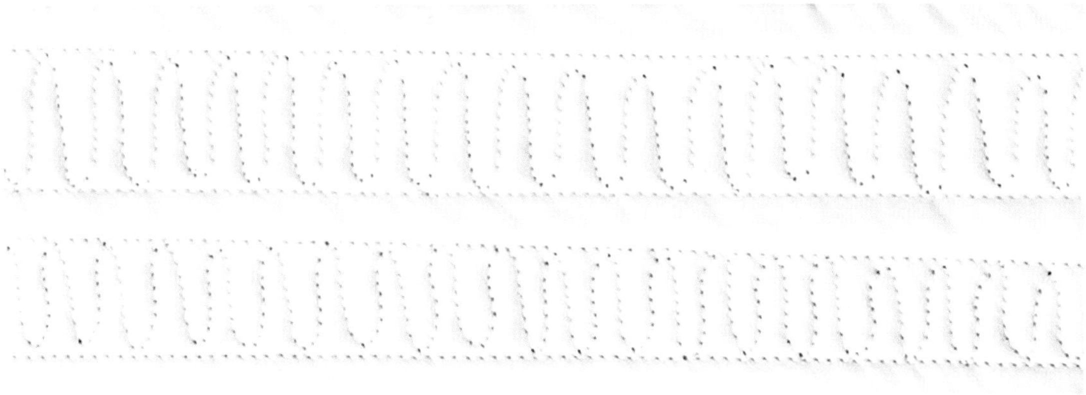

DIAMOND

The Diamond design can be great in a modern or traditional quilt. This design also can be a foundation for fun fillers.

STEP 1 · *Measure the width of the border; this will determine the size of the diamonds. For this sample, we will base the design on a 2˝ border.*

STEP 2 · *Mark straight lines through the border every 2˝.*

STEP 3 · *Starting at the inside point on the left end of the border, stitch a straight line to the lower marked point, then up to the next upper point.*

Repeat this process until you've stitched the entire length of the border.

1 & 2

3

STEP 4 • *When you get to the other end of the border, travel in a straight line to the opposite edge. From there, stitch diagonal lines from point-to-point to finish the diamond design.*

4

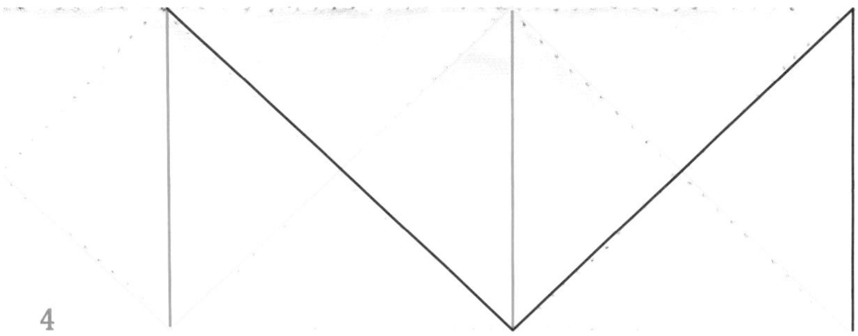

Diamond Variation

To emphasize the diamonds, stitch heavy filler in the triangles.

DIAMONDS INSIDE

This is a fun play off the Diamond design (page 108). To stitch this design, you'll first need to follow the steps for the Diamond design.

★ Natalia's Tip

Do not spritz away the blue marked lines from the diamond design before starting this design. You'll need those marking lines.

STEP 1 • *Beginning at the left inner point, stitch a straight line to the blue marked dot, ¼˝ inside the outside point. To avoid extra marking, use the edge of the machine quilting ruler as a guide.*

STEP 2 • *From that point, stitch a straight line to the right inside point of the diamond. Repeat the previous steps until you've completely filled in the diamonds, top and bottom.*

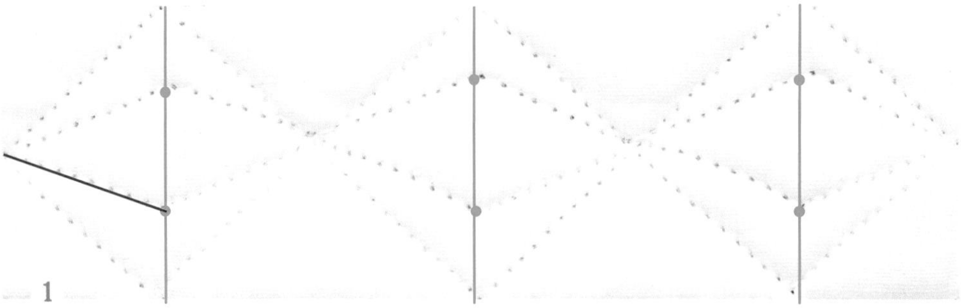

1

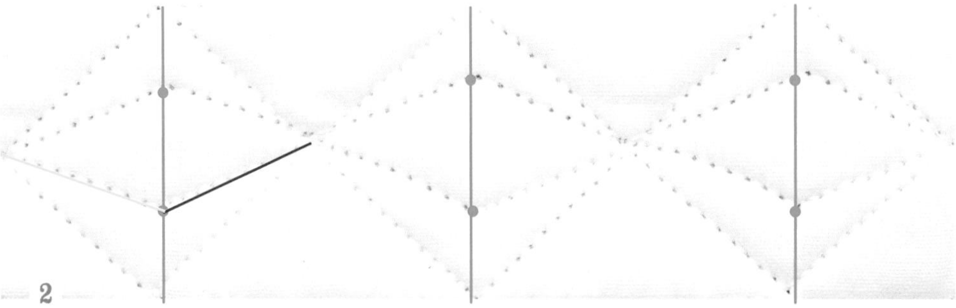

2

ZIPPER

The Zipper design is a great design for a smaller border, perfect for a stop border or other narrow border.

STEP 1 • *Begin by using a blue water-soluble pen to mark a line every 1˝.*

STEP 2 • *From the upper left point, stitch a straight line to the next lower marked point.*

STEP 3 • *From the lower point, stitch a straight line to the next upper point. Repeat this process until you've stitched a zipper all the way through the border.*

Spritz away the blue marks.

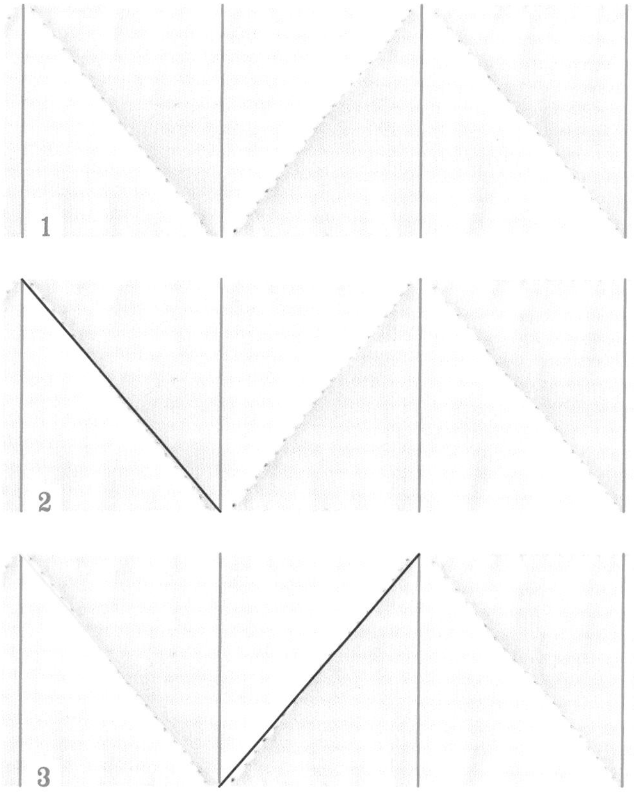

Allover DESIGNS

These designs can cover your entire quilt top, edge to edge. But many are versatile enough to be used as background fillers as well, or even as border designs. They will add lovely texture to your quilt without overpowering your patchwork. When you stitch an allover design, be sure to quilt the repeating pattern evenly over the whole quilt to make your quilt look good.

CRACKLE

The Crackle design can be used as an edge-to-edge design or even as a background filler. On the right quilt, it could even be used as a border design.

1

STEP 1 • *Begin by stitching a straight line about 1˝ long.*

STEP 2 • *Change directions and stitch a second straight line.*

2

STEP 3 • *Repeat the previous steps stitching random straight lines in various directions, keeping the lines all about 1˝ long.*

MAZE

The Maze design is very forgiving! Have fun with it.

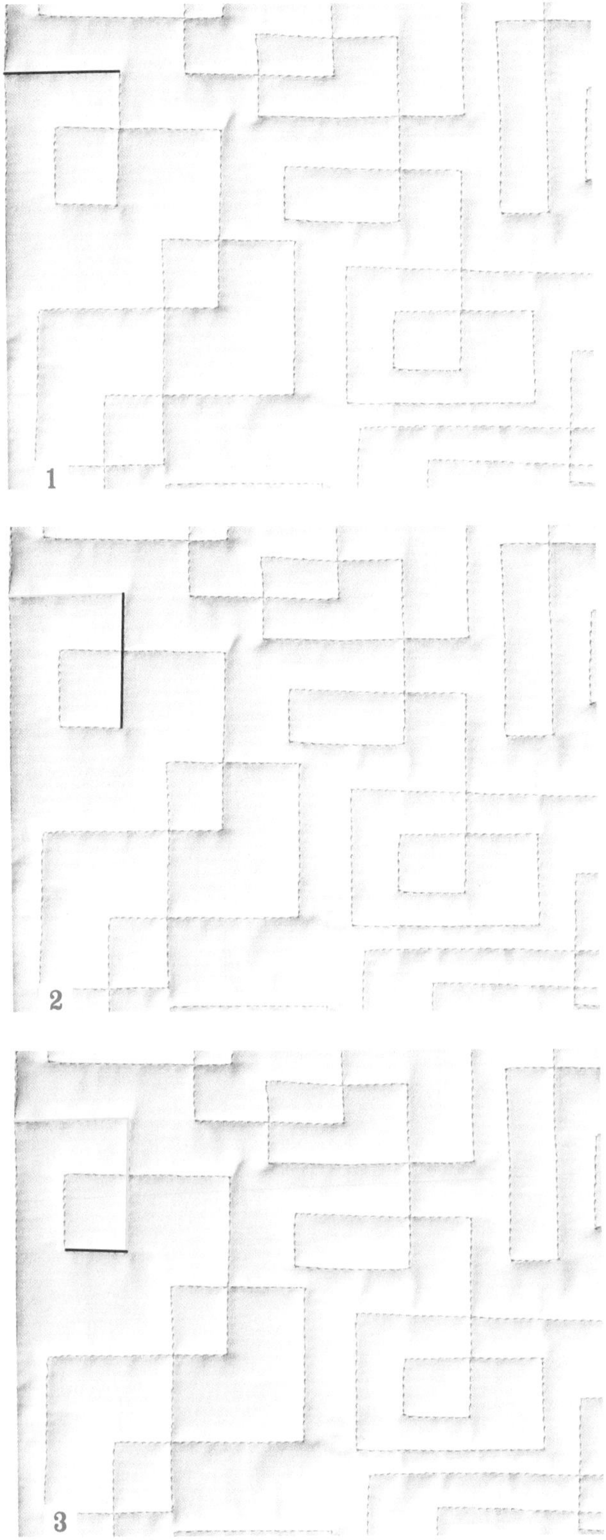

STEP 1 • *Beginning at the edge of the quilting area, stitch a straight line about 2˝ long.*

STEP 2 • *Turn a 90° angle and stitch a second straight line about 2˝ long.*

STEP 3 • *Turn a second 90° angle and stitch another straight line, stitch this line about 1˝ long.*

STEP 4 • *Keep stitching random boxes. You can cross over your original stitch lines at any point.*

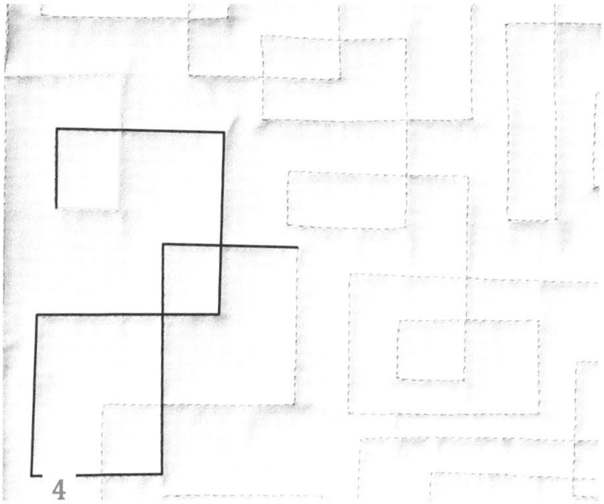

★ *Natalia's Tip*

For the best overall results with this design, just keep the density of the quilting consistent. If you're quilting heavy in one area, make all the quilting heavy. If you're quilting lighter, make all the quilting lighter.

ANGULAR

Angular is great as a background filler or allover design. The design is heavy, and you do have to be thinking ahead to get out of where you've stitched, but the overall result is worth the extra work.

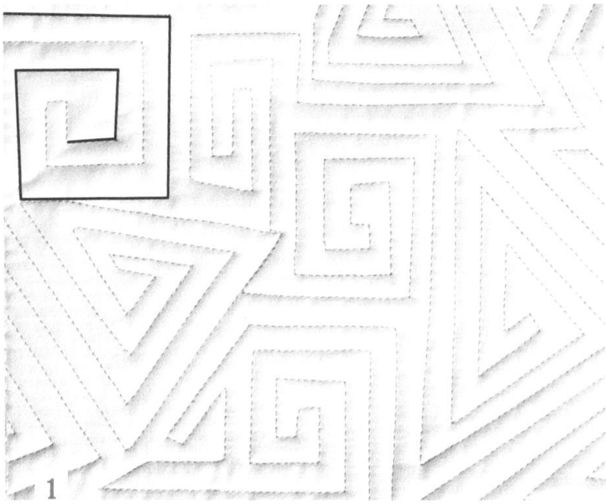

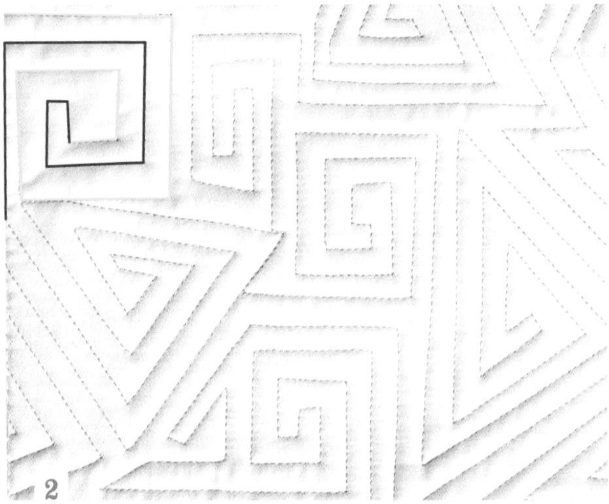

STEP 1 • *Begin by stitching a square spiral. Stitch into the center of the square but leave enough space to get back out.*

STEP 2 • *Stitch a second square spiral, moving out of the first one.*

STEP 3 • *When you exit the first square, spiral stitch a triangle shape. Spiral into the center but leave enough open space to stitch back out.*

STEP 4 • *Stitch a second triangle spiral, stitching out of the first one.*

STEP 5 • *Repeat previous steps, stitching square and triangle spirals until you've filled in the quilted area completely.*

★ Natalia's Tip

When quilting this design, you can occasionally feel stuck. If you ever do, echoing is your friend. Simply echo, even a few times until you can get to a new place to start a new square or triangle.

TEXTURED GRID

This design is so much fun to quilt and creates really cool dimension. It would look great as a background filler or allover design.

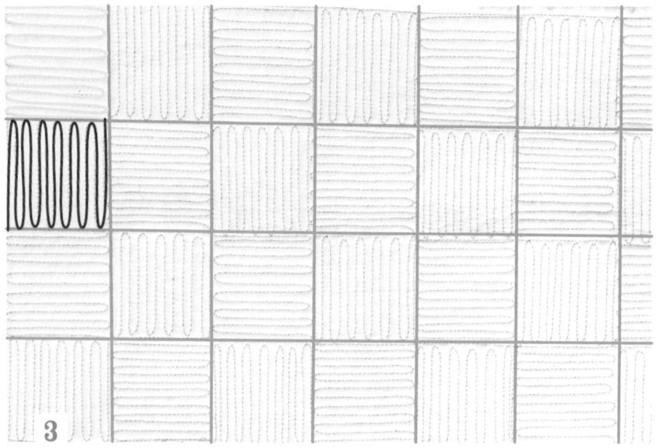

STEP 1 • *Use a blue water-soluble pen to mark a grid across the quilting area.*

★ Natalia's Tip

The scale of the grid will determine how heavy you'd like your machine quilting. For a larger quilt, I'd use larger spacing, like 2˝. For a smaller quilt, I'd use spacing that is about 1˝.

STEP 2 • *Beginning in the upper left corner, stitch small straight lines back and forth until you've filled in the square completely.*

STEP 3 • *Move to the square below and fill in with small straight lines, this time stitching in the opposite direction from the first block.*

STEP 4 • *Repeat the previous steps, working up and down until you've filled in the quilting area completely with the grid pattern.*

SQUARE STIPPLE

The Square Stipple design is similar to Crackle (page 113). However, with this design, the lines are all horizontal and vertical. And unlike the Maze design (page 116), the lines never cross over themselves.

STEP 1 • *Begin by stitching a straight horizontal line about 1˝ long.*

STEP 2 • *Turn a 90° angle and stitch a second straight line about ¾˝ long.*

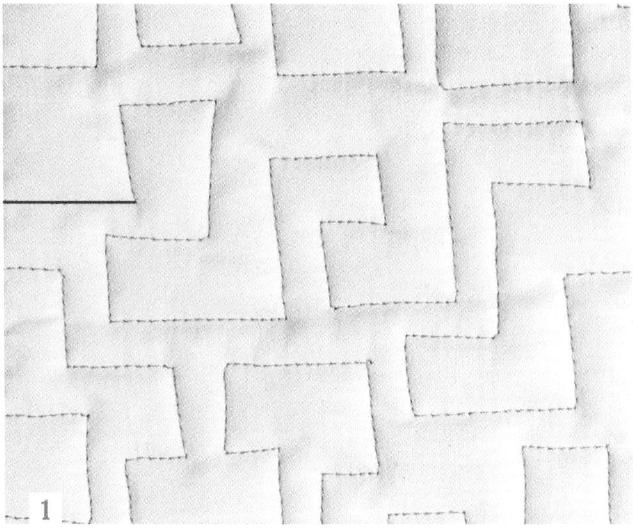

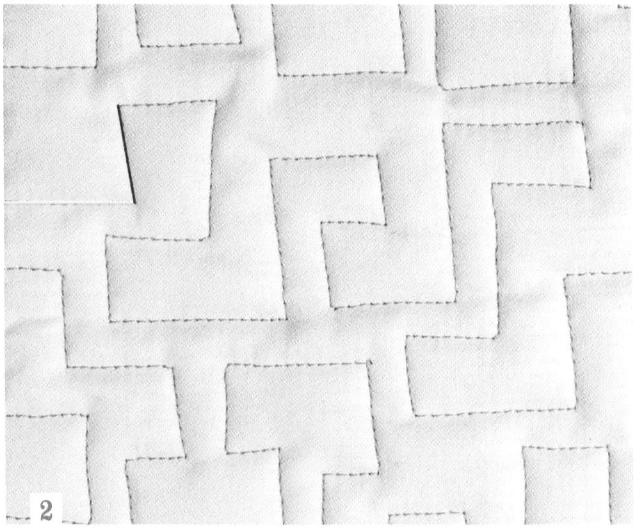

STEP 3 • *Turn another 90° angle and stitch a third straight line. Repeat this process, stitching straight lines that vary in length, but keeping them no more than 2˝ long. Continue stitching this pattern until the quilting area is covered completely.*

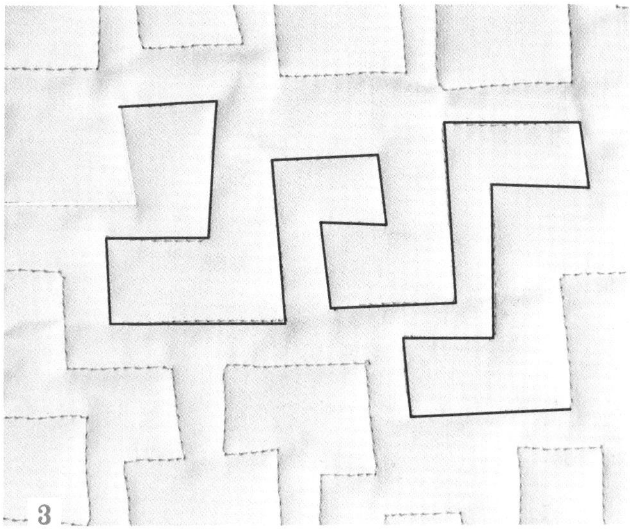

ABSTRACT LINES

This design can be really fun to quilt!

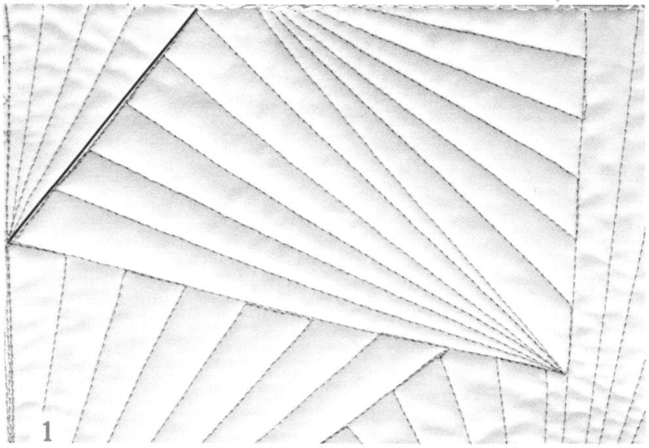

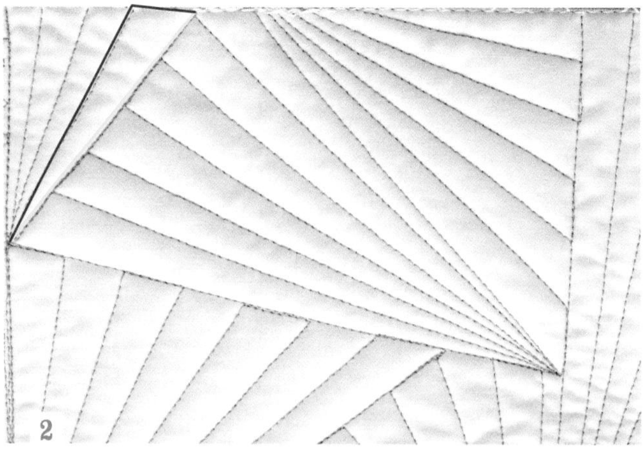

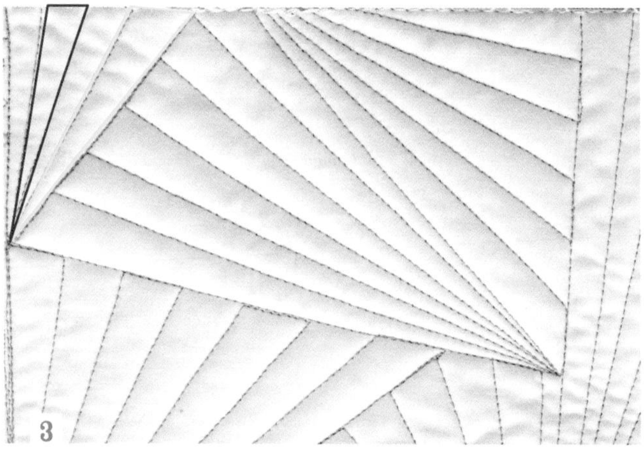

STEP 1 • *Beginning on the left side of the quilt, about 3˝ from the top, stitch a straight line to the top of the quilt, about 2˝ from the left side of the quilt, to create a triangle.*

STEP 2 • *Stitch back up to a point that is even with the top of the design, but about ½˝ from the previous point. Turn and stitch over another ½˝, then stitch a straight line back to the original starting point.*

STEP 3 • *Stitch another straight line back to the top of the design, traveling across the top of the design and back to the starting point to fill in the corner.*

STEP 4 • *From the starting point, stitch a straight diagonal line toward the right, about 3˝ long. From that point, stitch a straight line back to the top of the previous triangle, creating a new triangle.*

★ *Natalia's Tip*

Don't stress about the length of these lines; the more random the sizes of the triangles, the better the design will look overall.

STEP 5 • *From the upper point, stitch a straight line to the previous stitch diagonal line. Then travel along that line, moving to the right about ½˝. Then stitch a straight line back to the top point.*

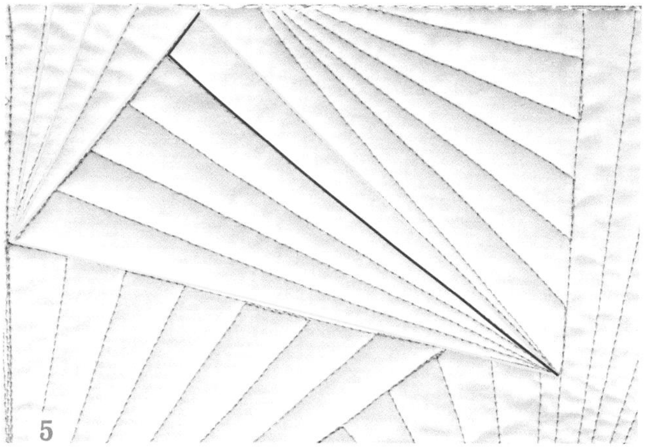

STEP 6 • *Repeat previous steps, creating triangles and then filling the triangles in with straight lines that are spaced about ½˝ apart at the widest points.*

BERNINA

About the AUTHOR

Natalia Whiting Bonner has enjoyed piecing quilt tops for more than twenty years. She learned how to quilt on her conventional home machine. She felt good about it but decided that if she really wanted to take her quilting to the next level, she needed to invest in a longarm machine. In 2007, when she was pregnant with her daughter, she got the crazy idea to quit her job as a dental assistant and become a longarm quilter. Without really knowing what a longarm machine was, she spent a day at a longarm dealer's shop and walked out after purchasing a Gammill machine. Natalia's passion for quilting and being creative has grown each day since.

Whether it's working on an intense show quilt or a simple baby quilt, Natalia has become a real quilting addict. She teaches at quilt guilds and shows, including Road to California, QuiltCon, and MQX, and has filmed TV shows with Nancy Zieman and Jodie Davis. She has won numerous awards for her work and has been featured on the Moda Bake Shop website; in the magazines *Quiltmaker* and in *American Patchwork & Quilting*; and in books, such as *Fresh Fabric Treats*, *Modern Blocks*, *Sweet Celebrations with the Moda Bake Shop Chefs*, and *Modern Quilts from the Blogging Universe*. Natalia is the author of *Beginner's Guide to Free-Motion Quilting*, *Next Steps in Machine Quilting*, and *Visual Guide to Free-Motion Quilting Feathers*, and the coauthor of *Modern One-Block Quilts* and *Cabin Fever*.

Natalia is a Gammill Quilt Artist and Craftsy Instructor and has designed fabric for Moda Fabrics.

Visit Natalia online and follow on social media!

Website: piecenquilt.com

Facebook: /piecenquilt

Instagram: @nataliabonner

Twitter: @piecenquilt

YouTube: /nataliabonner

Also by Natalia Bonner: